MOURNING UNDER GLASS

REFLECTIONS ON A SON'S MURDER

NAFTALI MOSES

In memory of my beloved son,

Avraham David Moses

and

*For all those touched
by the horrors of hatred*

CONTENTS

ACKNOWLEDGMENTS

This book is the result of both personal tragedy and communal support. Its publication was aided by a generous grant given to me by the One Family Fund. One Family is dedicated to helping Israeli terror victims rebuild, recover and heal. I thank them profusely for all the good works they do.

My good friend and talented photographer, Abba Richman, designed the book and its cover.

Another friend, neighbor, and writer, Channah Koppel, edited the original manuscript into a better final product. My longtime friend Mindy Kornberg did the copy editing and offered many suggestions that improved the manuscript. My friend Yisrael Smith did a final proofreading. Many thanks.

FORWARD

One fine summer night in July, 1984, just six weeks after graduating from college, I stayed up until daybreak packing away all my earthly belongings. Most went into the attic of the small Long Island house where I had grown up. The rest was stuffed into a large backpack. A large cardboard box held my bicycle. By midday, I was on an El Al flight to Israel comfortably sleeping the sleep of a young man confident in his life's newly chosen trajectory.

I was on my way to make a new life in the Promised Land. I grew up in a deeply Jewish, but not overly religious, family and had always felt some connection to Israel. After a six-week visit to Israel in my sixteenth summer, though, the country had captured my attention to the extent that I felt sure that one day I would make it my home. So, six years later, holding a BA in religious studies (with a complementary minor in unemployment), I had registered for a year of yeshivah study in Jerusalem. Unlike most of my fellow American students, I had only purchased a one-way ticket. I wanted to stay.

And I did. I eventually studied and taught in several different yeshivahs, served in the IDF, married, had two wonderful sons, divorced from their mother, remarried and added two beautiful girls to the Moses family line. I would eventually complete a doctorate in medical history, writing my thesis on brain-death in Israel society. All this while living in the midst of one of the twentieth century's most profoundly successful, yet deeply discordant, social experiments ever undertaken — the State of Israel.

This book is not a record of the past 27 years, though. It focuses on just one year of my life: a year of mourning after my firstborn son was cruelly murdered in a Jerusalem terrorist attack.

Avraham David was a beautiful child. He had sparkling blue eyes set into a sweet face, and long blond hair. Even as an infant, he was unusually alert, taking in everything around him. He grew up in a home in which he was deeply loved by his two parents even though their marriage ended before he was eight. In school he was a quick learner, but like many highly intelligent boys, socially awkward. By the time he reached high school, he had decided to dedicate himself to Torah study. He had committed remarkable amounts of material to memory; he was able to recite entire Orders of Mishnah by heart and could catch mistakenly quoted biblical passages in published texts. The first year that he spent in his yeshivah high school, Yeshivat Yerusahlayim L'Tze'irim ("Yashlatz" for short), was wonderful for him. Aside from having to adjust to noisy dorm life, he loved every minute. He flourished. I remember his grandfather asking him on the phone from America if he liked school. "Like it? I love it!" was his response.

But by the next year, in tenth grade, something was amiss. In this last school year of his too-short life, at the age of sixteen, he was getting up before dawn every morning and spending nearly sixteen hours a day immersed in studying Talmud, Jewish law and Bible. His devotion—to study, to prayer, to living his life in exacting accordance to Jewish law, came, it seemed to me, from a place that was clouded with anxiety and darkness. I had long talks with him about his solitude, about his decision to stop attending classes and to learn only with his study partners. I wondered out loud, together with him, where the real joy that should be found in intellectual and spiritual growth had gone. I missed his smile, I missed laughing together. There was something too serious for sixteen about him. And, after several long and serious conversations, I believe that he came to recognize this, too.

Avraham David spent the evening that preceded the night of his murder talking to the dean of his yeshivah about his life—about growing up in the two homes of his divorced parents, about his future, about finding his place in the world. His school's social worker, with whom he had already met several times, told me that he greeted her the morning of his death with a big smile. He told her that he wanted to figure out what was troubling him and move on. He was ready—and this is no easy thing for a teenage boy to admit – to accept her help.

But he would never again get the chance to sit in her small office.

One of the things that saddens me most is that the timing of Avraham David's terrible death never allowed him to regain the joy that had been his growing up. I remember hiking with him in a wadi not far from our house during his last summer. Although close to Jerusalem, Nahal Katlev offers a suprising degree of solitude once you descend down into the wadi bed. We hiked and explored the ruins of one of the original 19th-century Jerusalem-Jaffa train stations. After turning around, we began the steep ascent out of the valley. Avraham David smiled at me as I huffed with effort and offered to take the knapsack I was carrying. He shouldered the bag, smiled at me again and took off uphill quickly leaving me behind. As I came to the end of the climb, sweating and panting, there he was waiting for me at the top near the trailhead looking at his watch with a big grin on his face. We had hiked and biked together since he was only two—and he had finally bested his old man. I laughed with him as he announced how many minutes he had already been sitting in the sun watching for my arrival. We strolled together back to the car happy to be together, each of us happy to witness a boy's growing-up.

Only a few months later, on a rainy Jerusalem night, we would be sitting in my car, he and I, talking about whether he would remain at Yashlatz at all, why he had stopped attending classes and why he had spent a few weeks trying to subsist on mostly bread and water while keeping up a grueling study schedule. Was he on his way to becoming one of our generation's Torah luminaries? I wasn't sure. I was a worried father wondering what was becoming of his son.

In the end, what he became was another victim of Arab terror. A "martyr" killed only because he was a Jew living in the Jewish state and learning Torah. As much as I mourn Avraham David, the boy he was, I also mourn his lost chance; I mourn for what he might have become. Even if it was only a contented, smiling youth once again. Where his soul resides now—in the upper reaches of heaven reserved for the innocent martyrs of our people—perhaps, in a way, he is just that once more.

> *Readers interested in visual memory are invited to visit the website tragic-death.com where a short slide show featuring Avraham David can be viewed.*

CHAPTER ONE:
THE DARKEST NIGHT

And cursed be he who says: Revenge!
Revenge like this, revenge for the blood of a small child
Even the devil has not created...

HAIM NAHMAN BIALIK, "ON THE SLAUGHTER"

Ala Abu Dheim was a 20-year-old Jerusalem school bus driver. He worked for his family's company, ferrying special education students to school. His father, a building engineer, had for years operated a minibus line, successfully bidding on municipal tenders for student transport. On March 6, 2008, after a normal workday, Abu Dheim, the son, parked one of the company vans outside a religious studies college, the Mercaz HaRav Yeshivah, and walked through its open gates. It was nearly 8:10 pm. Carrying a large box in his arms, he set it down in the school's courtyard, just across from the dormitory entrance. There he opened his package and began to make his last delivery.

Out of the box came a Kalashnikov assault rifle. It had been purchased some time before in Dura, one of the small villages between Hebron and Be'er Sheva, for "criminal" use. In General

Security Services lingo, this means intra-Arab crime—drugs, car theft, and the like. Although Abu Dheim still lived with his parents, he was engaged to be married and his dabbling in petty theft may have been a way to supplement the salary his father paid him. He had already done a few months in prison. On this day, though, his weapon would find a higher use, one that would make him a holy man, a holy martyr—a *shahid*—in the eyes of his Arab brethren who would dance in the streets when they heard what he had done.

Thursday night in the yeshivah is a busy time. A week of learning is drawing to a close. Most of the students stay up well past midnight studying. Some don't sleep at all—a custom called *mishmar* ("guard duty" of a spiritual nature). Some want to review their week's learning, and some want to make one last push ahead before Shabbat, the day of rest.

This particular Thursday was a bit different, however. It was the first day of the Jewish month of Adar. Adar is the last month of the Jewish calendar and host to its most boisterously joyful holiday, Purim. The beginning of the month is marked in all yeshivahs with parties. "When Adar begins, we increase the happiness," says the Talmud. Traditionally, yeshivah students dance, sing, and practical-joke their way through the two weeks from the first of Adar until Purim itself, when the festivities reach their apogee of alcohol-fueled celebration. For Purim is the one day in the traditional Jewish calendar when drinking is actually encouraged.

The Yashlatz students, in their high school building adjacent to the Mercaz HaRav campus, were busy clearing tables and chairs from the study hall and stringing up decorations in anticipation of the party scheduled to begin after evening prayers. Some had gone to the Old City for a special monthly prayer rally held on the eve of each new moon and had not yet returned. Some were on a school trip and would be pulling up in a pair of buses a few minutes after Abu Dheim arrived.

Yashlatz is one of religious Zionism's top institutions. The students, boisterous young teenagers, are expected to devote hours every day to Torah study. Many of the students learn late into the night, mastering another page, another tractate, another book devoted to Jewish thought and practice. The *beit midrash* (study hall) is the school's center. Here, day in and day out, sitting on well-worn benches with their books resting on wooden lecterns, these high school boys diligently argue over the points of laws recorded in their large Talmuds. During their secular studies, some of these same boys can be found fast asleep, either in their dorm beds or at their classroom desks. Some relax by exploring Jerusalem's many (kosher) treasures—wandering her alleyways, hiking in her hills. Several of the most serious students are officially excused from time-consuming secular subjects like advanced math and English so that they can concentrate exclusively on their religious studies.

My son Avraham David had decided not to let any of the extracurricular Purim activities interfere with his Torah studies. He and his friend Segev Avihayil, both serious sixteen-year-olds in tenth grade, had made up to learn together in the Mercaz HaRav library that evening. The library, home to one of Jerusalem's better collections of opened-stacked *sifrei kodesh* (Judaica, literally "holy books") is accessible to the general public. On Thursdays especially, it is usually filled not only with the yeshivah's college-aged students, but also with neighborhood residents who take advantage of its quiet and the available desk space to study for part of the evening.

A neighbor of mine studied on Thursdays in a rabbinic ordination class for older professionals which was held in a classroom above the library. They were lacking a tenth man needed to form a *minyan* (quorum) for the evening prayers. Somebody sent down to the library and asked one of the high school students to come up and join them for the short fifteen-minute service, which he did. A dozen or so older students were in one of the two small classrooms at the eastern edge of the library waiting for a lesson to begin.

As it was a Thursday, my other son, eleven-year-old Elisha Dan, was home with me in Efrat. (Half of the week Elisha Dan lives next door with his mother, my ex-wife Rivkah, and half the week he lives with me.) My wife Leah was working in her office and our two young daughters were already asleep in their beds. Elisha Dan and I were reviewing the Book of Joel together—reading about the coming of the "day of the Lord"—for an upcoming test. Since his older brother had left the year before to the high school dormitory, Elisha Dan and I had been spending more time together, just the two of us. Whether it was studying Talmud, or playing tennis, or doing a home fix-it project which I had saved to work on with him, once he arrived at my house for his half-week every Wednesday afternoon, we were usually involved in some joint activity. That evening, we sat in my small workroom, surrounded by books and bicycle tools (artifacts of my two main interests), with our Bibles open.

That same Thursday evening, Yonadav Haim Hirshfeld stood talking with two younger Yashlatz students outside of the Mercaz HaRav dormitories. He had graduated from Yashlatz the previous year and decided to continue his studies at the advanced yeshivah next door, Mercaz HaRav. Yonadav Haim had just returned early from the Old City prayer rally. The backpack slung over his shoulder held his beloved wooden flute and well-worn Mishnah. Tzvi Kaufman and Shimon Balzam noticed the man carrying a large box just as he set it down. They joked, "Who ordered the TV?"

Abu Dheim had drilled with his Kalashnikov in the valleys south of Hebron—he'd practiced and learned how to quickly switch magazines. As he lifted the rifle out of the box and brought the stock up to his shoulder, his training paid off. There, right in front of him stood three Jews. *Pop-pop-pop*. But they didn't fall. He hit them at point blank range but they didn't fall. They ran off, into the building. He turned to his right, there was another. *Pop-pop-pop*. At last, a dead Jew. This was Ro'ee Roth—a squarely built 18-year-old who held a brown belt in ju-jitsu. It was his first year at Mercaz HaRav. Ro'ee collapsed in a bloody puddle on the white hewn-stone pavement.

Yonaton Yitshak Eldar, a tenth-grader, heard the shots just as he had exited the library where he had been studying. As he turned to run, Abu Dheim shot him in the back. He fell dead, not far from where Ro'ee Roth lay.

Abu Dheim missed Tzvi completely. Even though they were wounded, Shimon and Yonadav Haim managed to run inside the yeshivah dormitory building. Shimon and Tzvi headed in one direction, while Yonadav turned in another. He headed down the stairs bleeding badly and there collapsed. Before Abu Dheim had emptied his first magazine, Yonadav Haim, the first Jew he shot that night, was dead. Abu Dheim didn't follow them inside. Instead, he turned to his right. Now the large plate glass windows of the Mercaz HaRav library were on his left. A little further on was the door. He turned left and entered.

Inside the neighboring Yashlatz building, some of the high school students heard what they took to be the popping of firecrackers—a usual accompaniment to pre-Purim festivities. The yeshivah's headmaster, the even-tempered, sixty-something-year-old Rabbi Yerahmiel Weiss heard them too. In his daily ten minute talk to the entire student body after morning prayers, he had recently mentioned, as he had in his pre-Adar talk for the past twenty years, the need for restraint in the coming days of merry-making. An avuncular, yet busy man (he is responsible for the spiritual growth and physical well-being of 250 teenage boys) he might not have been surprised that his call for calm had not been heeded. *Pop-pop-pop.* But Rabbi Weiss quickly realized that these weren't the sounds of Purim fireworks. These were shots ringing out from somewhere close by. He yelled at the students nearby to run for cover as he did the same.

Pop-pop-pop. Inside the library, the boys who were learning stopped for a moment, wondering what the noise was. It took them a few seconds to realize that it wasn't just Purim fireworks. As the realization that they were hearing gun shots took hold, Abu Dheim approached the door.

Upon entering the library, one is directly across from the librarian's desk, situated about half-way into the room's depth. A bit to the right there are some well-worn computers. In line with the desk, to its left, and filling much of the library's space, are the open stacks of books. On simple brown metal shelving sit thousands of Hebrew books, ranging from Talmudic texts to contemporary Jewish law. In front of the stacks, to the left of the doorway, are tables and chairs. Some are set together, forming islands in the middle of the space; some are set against the windows fronting the library.

As Abu Dheim entered the room, the Jews sitting at the tables were already scattering. No matter. His rifle came up and he hit one who hadn't even looked up from his studies. Doron Maharate, born in Ethiopia, left high school in the 11th grade to study at Mercaz HaRav. He dreamed of ordination and longed to become a religious leader for other Ethiopian Jews whose place in Israeli society was not easy. Quickly, Abu Dheim ended his dreams.

Pop-pop-pop. My neighbor's rabbinical class, in the room above the library, had just finished saying their evening prayers. These were shots! My neighbor, Moise, usually carried a pistol but tonight he had left it at home. He and his classmates quickly barricaded the door with tables, placing them against the door and then sitting themselves against the opposite wall. This way they could keep the tables pressed to the door by pushing against them with their legs.

Pop-pop-pop. The dozen students in the classroom off the library slammed the door shut. In shock, they held the door shut while fervently whispering psalms. Twice, they would quickly open the door to admit other students who had crawled across the library floor seeking somewhere, anywhere, to hide. Once, they would hold their collective breaths as the door handle to their small room rattled in the hand of Abu Dheim.

Pop-pop-pop. Captain David Shapiro was at home, on leave from duty as a combat officer with the paratroopers. The twenty-nine-year-old rents a small apartment across the street from Mercaz HaRav. He had spent his high school years in Yashlatz. His pregnant wife had just put one of their two sons to bed. "Fireworks?" he thought for a second. "No, this is gun fire!" He grabbed his rifle, jammed in a magazine and ran out the door.

19

In the library, people had fled like so many mice into the stacks. Methodically, though, Abu Dheim began to hunt them down. Lying on the floor in the classroom to the right of the door, holding the door closed with all their strength, were the students who had been waiting for their rabbi to begin his class. One dialed Magen David Adom – the Israeli Red Cross—and whispered into his cell phone that they were under attack. Outside the door, they could hear shots ringing out. Suddenly, they heard a piercing scream, an animal-like cry, a wailing which continued for seconds which felt like hours followed by an even more terrifying silence. Then, another round of shots rang out. Segev called to his friend who remained seated. It took Avraham David, blessed with high intelligence, but an often frustrating deliberateness, a moment to register what was happening. "Moses! Moses! Move!" Avraham David followed the other fleeing students to the narrow spaces between the crowded shelves. Abu Dheim walked slowly through the stacks. Crouching between them were the Jews. He emptied magazine after magazine into them. His shots passed through the bodies of my son and his friend Segev, scarring the hard stone floor. In all, he would kill five in the library.

As the blood ran across the stone tile, a small boy suddenly jumped up into Abu Dheim's line of vision. This was Elhanan Cohen, a sixteen-year-old tenth grader. Abu Dheim squeezed the trigger. Nothing happened. The rifle had jammed. In the second required for Abu Dheim to pull back on the bolt to clear it, Elhanan grabbed the barrel, which was so hot that it seared the flesh of his palm, and pushed past Abu Dheim. Elhanan's younger cousin, Neriah, was already dead, the blood running out of his lifeless body and across the floor tiles. Yochai Lifshitz, tall and thin like both his parents, due to graduate high school in a few months, also lay dead among the library stacks.

Abu Dheim walked back toward the entranceway. He reached for the door handle of what looked like a closet. Inside, the students didn't dare breathe. They silently strained against the door, watching as the handle shook and the door rattled. They envisioned their end—the angel of death bursting through the inch of wood that stood between them and the man doing all the shooting and killing they had been listening to these past minutes. Then ... nothing. The door fell silent.

Captain David Shapiro ran toward the yeshivah. His eyes scanning the street, he held his M16 loosely in his practiced hands, allowing it to swing back and forth across his chest in time with each stride, ready to be cocked, shifted into position and fired in an instant. A patrol car was already outside the yeshivah gate when he arrived. A rookie team of a patrolman and -woman had been just down the street when the call about an attack in progress came over the radio. They made a u-turn and jumped out of the car. The policewoman ran down the street in the direction from which they had just come in order to stop an approaching bus from getting any closer to the yeshivah where shots could be heard. The policeman was crouched down, trying to decide what to do. Unbeknownst to either him or Captain Shapiro, a married Mercaz HaRav student named Rabbi Yitzhak Dadon, armed with a pistol, had crawled out onto a small balcony on the second floor of the yeshivah building. The balcony looked out over a courtyard to the glass facade of the library.

As Dadon lay waiting, trying to peer through the glass wall of the library for a clear shot at Abu Dheim, he suddenly spotted movement below him. This was Shapiro who had left the rookie policeman behind and was advancing toward the shooting, trying to stay as low as possible. Dadon was worried that the figure below him might mistake him for a terrorist and shoot at him. He called out his own name in Hebrew.

Abu Dheim had rattled the classroom door, tried to push it open, and found it shut tight. As far as he knew, he was done with all the Jews in this library. By now, though, the sound of police sirens could be heard in the library. Reflected off the glass front of the library was the red and blue glow of flashing police lights. He turned toward the door and stepped outside. Dadon pulled himself back as the terrorist came out of the library. He pressed himself to the floor of the balcony as the shooter unloaded a clip of rounds in the air, seemingly not aiming at anyone. The terrorist, wearing a flak jacket, its pouches full of rifle magazines, stepped back into the library and pulled the door shut, while still facing the outside. Dadon lifted himself up a bit, leaned over the edge of the balcony and emptied his pistol in the direction of the shooter. Shapiro, armed with an assault rifle, opened fire a split-second later. Abu Dheim was hit. A pistol shot had grazed his skull. He staggered. Then heavy rifle rounds, hitting him like well-delivered punches, pushed him back into the library. Another, another. With his rifle still slung over his neck, unspent magazines tucked into his combat vest and two pistols still holstered, Abu Dheim fell to the floor, face-down, dead.

Shapiro quickly made his way inside. He had seen the terrorist go down. The thought that the terrorist might have booby-trapped his own body went through his mind. He gingerly stepped over the dead body lying in the doorway and made a quick scan of the library. Behind him, two more experienced police detectives arrived. He could hear the screaming sirens of ambulances pulling up on the street below. There in front of Shapiro, slumped over the the open books he had been studying a few minutes earlier, lay the body of Doron Maharate. Making his way deeper into the room, stepping through pools of blood covering the floor, he came upon body after body slumped among the stacks. One of them weakly lifted a hand in his direction. This was Naftali Sheetrit. He had been hit by five bullets and was somehow still struggling for life. Shapiro turned, ran outside, and yelled the boy's location at one of the medics who was jumping from an ambulance which had barely stopped. "Get to him first, he's still alive!" Naftali, a diminutive 14-year-old, would live because the mobile ICU driver who raced to scoop up his small body cut five precious minutes off the rush to the hospital by taking him to the closer Shaare Zedek Medical Center instead of down the hill to Hadassah Ein Kerem.

Now, accompanied by the two police detectives, Shapiro re-entered the building and began to search for another terrorist, which was always a possibility. As more forces arrived, they would make a room-by-room search of the premises—here discovering some students hiding under their beds, there breaking down a door to an unoccupied room, there coming across those who had barricaded themselves in the library classroom.

As the injured were still being evacuated, my phone rang, interrupting my study session with Elisha Dan. It was Avraham David's stepfather calling me from Jerusalem. Had I heard about a terrorist attack at Mercaz HaRav? No I hadn't. My son and I closed our Bibles and turned on the internet and radio news.

At first, the news reported only some wounded, and maybe the death of the terrorist himself. In the surreal world of Israeli terror, this was nothing to get overly excited about. My wife had once called me from the Hebrew University campus where she was studying for the summer and described a flow of bloodied students running from one of the cafeterias. "What should I do?" she asked.

"Follow them—they're running to safer ground." An employee had just detonated a bomb among the students—Jews, Christians, and Muslims—who were sitting down to lunch. By evening, my wife was safely home, preparing to attend the funeral of one of her classmates the following day.

I tried my son's cell phone. No answer. This was not surprising as my son was not the type to keep his phone on (or even with him) when he was studying. He would sometimes return a call a day later when he remembered to check for messages. Still watching the news, I called some school numbers, without success. We saw on the news that the whole neighborhood around the yeshiva was being sealed off. The initial reports spoke of a party in the yeshivah having been the focus of the attack. However, as my son studied in the adjacent high school, and not the yeshivah for college-aged men, I still wasn't too worried. Elisha Dan and I followed the updates in my study, waiting for his brother to call. My wife sat in her home office trying to keep herself distracted as we filled her in from time to time. My ex-wife, in Jerusalem for the evening with her husband, called and we agreed to keep each other posted when we heard from Avraham David.

Finally, the phone rang. It was a young-sounding voice asking for Avraham David. "No, he's not here. Who is this?" It was one of his classmates calling from school. I realized the truth as I put it to the boy who was trying his best to sound nonchalant, "He's missing, isn't he?" He had to admit that this was true.

As more of the story broke, the news was growing worse—students had been wounded, some killed, an angry crowd had formed outside the yeshivah, maybe there was a second terrorist still at large. The well-oiled Israeli terror-response machinery was swinging into action. Phone numbers of the hospitals to which the wounded had been evacuated were announced on the air. My 11-year-old and I began making more phone calls. We spoke to a woman who sounded like anybody's seventy-year-old aunt at Shaare Zedek Medical Center and to a younger operator at Hadassah Hospital. Neither could help us. "Check back later," we were told. "Nobody by the name of Moses has been admitted." The line was busy. "No Moses." But…at some point in the half-dozen conversations with these two women over the next hour we discovered that there were some unidentified wounded. Rivkah discovered that someone knew of Avraham David's plans to study that evening with his friend Segev. She filled me in that Segev was also missing.

At 10:30 pm, the operator at Hadassah asked me to describe my son. They had an unidentified boy from the yeshivah there. "Skinny, still beardless, blond, blue eyes – about 5'7"."

"Hold please."

It would be a cliché to write that the minute she took to check our description seemed like hours. But—it didn't. My son and I were both calm. We waited, listened to some more news and watched the computer as websites were updated. She came back on the line.

"Does he have braces?"

"No."

"Then it's not him."

I mentioned that his friend was also missing, and that his friend, if I recalled correctly, did have braces. With this bit of news, she paused. "Listen, if you're telling me that two kids who were studying together are missing…well, I'm not supposed to tell you this, but…at Shaare Zedek, two unidentified victims were admitted. Maybe check there. Good luck."

The phone rang again. Its sound brought a wave of relief—it must be Avraham David. But it was the mother of another local boy who had gone to elementary school together with Avraham David and Segev. The three had moved on together to high school in Jerusalem. Sounding relieved to hear my voice, she asked me a question as if she already knew the obvious answer, "You've heard from Avraham David, right? My Avishay called already." The expected answer was part of the question – of course our children are safe. It's an assumption made by parents all the time. We wouldn't let our children out of our sight otherwise, would we? What could I say? "No, I haven't. He seems to be missing right now." And what does one say to *that*? (The next day Avishay's head of bushy red hair would catch my eye at the cemetery. He had been forced to choose between which one of his two friends' funerals he would attend, Avraham David's or Segev's. He cried enough for both.)

A good friend, Mindy, also called. She was a bit more hesitant in asking if everything was alright. I told her that I was off to the hospital to look for Avraham David. At this point I was certain that he and his friend were there. I had planned on leaving alone, but my 11-year-old, who had been manning the phones with me for the previous two hours, insisted that he was coming. I was in a rush and didn't want to argue. I told him, "Let's go," and grabbed my *tallit* and *tefillin* (needed for the next day's morning prayer), telling my wife that I was sure we would be in the hospital through the morning.

It was now 11:00 pm. I turned on the car radio. The first thing we heard on the news was that the attack had taken place in the library and not in the yeshivah building. The attack had occurred while a party was in progress in the yeshivah itself. The second report we heard was about two wounded victims who had been admitted to the hospital in critical condition, but were already out of danger. Now everything seemed to be falling into place. Of course, if the attack was in the library, that would explain how Avraham David and Segev had been wounded. Avraham David often studied there. I would usually meet him once a week for breakfast, picking him up after morning prayers from his regular table in the library. I imagined him there, at his regular spot right across from the door, immersed in study, waiting for our weekly walk down the block for croissants. Elisha Dan and I were certain that the report was describing Avraham David and Segev. We joked about the news of the seeming rapid recovery of the two who were wounded. I said that by the time we got to the hospital, Avraham David would be up, waiting for us in a bed and wearing a hospital gown. As Elisha Dan has commented several times since (with no small measure of pride), the half-hour drive to Jerusalem took us 12 minutes. I hadn't noticed how fast I was driving.

The entrance to the Shaare Zedek emergency room is tucked into a covered parking lot so that patients can be unloaded in an area protected from shelling or sniper fire, if it ever came to that. We parked a few yards away and walked over to the door. There were about a dozen people milling about. Some news crews were folding up their cameras. The excitement was over. My son and I confidently went up to the guard who had a list of names on a clipboard. "Is there a Moses listed?"

"No." "I was told that two unidentified patients were admitted."

The guard knew nothing about that. He shooed us away. For the first time that night I was genuinely puzzled. What to do now? I wanted to ask about Avraham David's friend Segev, but I couldn't remember his last name. Just then my ex-wife, Rivkah, and her husband, David Moriah, came walking up. (I had told them that I thought the boys were here.) Rivkah knew that Segev's last name was Avihayil. I mentioned the name to the guard and got the same response as I had with "Moses." But someone else had heard us mention Avihayil. A non-descript man with a light-brown mustache and knit kippah suddenly appeared, asking, "Who said *Avihayil*? Come with me." The four of us were led inside. My son and I were now confident that our search had ended.

I learned what "whisked away" means. Our guide ushered us quickly and silently down a maze of corridors, through one set of doors, then another, into some elevators, through another set of doors into what looked like some type of office-cum-waiting room. (On a later visit to the hospital I learned that this is the public relations reception area.) There, Segev's parents and some other family members of his were standing near a desk with some "plainclothes" hospital officials. They all turned as we entered the room. Seeing us, Segev's mother, her face torn between fear and relief, said, "It's not them." They had just been shown photos of the two boys who were in the operating room.

Now what? Somebody from Segev's family was working his cell phone. At this point no one wanted to say what options regarding our boys were left, although by now we had all heard that there had been casualties. I was again confused. The cell phone man turned to us and said that the dead had been identified. Neither of our sons was among them.

Everyone was confused. Where were the boys? Leaving the area to which we had been brought, my son and I wandered down to the emergency room again. Avraham David's stepfather was on his cell, trying to find out about the unidentified victim across town in Hadassah. Near the emergency room, off to the side, was a small office marked "social worker." Soon we found ourselves sitting with a middle-aged woman who tried to get through to the police for us. It was by now just after midnight. She succeeded and told us that the general practice in situations like this was to remove bodies to the Abu Kabir Forensic Institute near Tel Aviv for identification. "Maybe you should try to get to the yeshivah, just to rule out the worst, and save yourself a trip to Tel Aviv," she suggested.

Still wondering what my next step should be, I searched my cell phone for the number of someone from the yeshivah who might answer my call. I tried the number of Avraham David's old dorm counselor. I was surprised that someone actually picked up, as there had been no answer from any of the Yashlatz numbers for hours. Zvi Yehuda, a young man who studied filmmaking by day and ran one of the dormitories at night, listened calmly as I explained our situation. He suggested that I come to the yeshivah, where all the students and teachers had gathered. "Everybody's here. I'm sure that Avraham David is as well." I told David and Rivkah that I was going to go to the yeshivah. But David felt that that he had a lead on the Hadassah victim and wanted to go there. We decided to split up.

As we got into the car, my cell phone rang. It was my friend Mindy again, checking for news. I explained that we hadn't found him in the hospital. Tentatively, she asked, "Is that good?" This was the first moment that the very real possibility that it wasn't really hit home. I managed to answer, "I don't know," as I began to choke with emotion at the thought of where this search could actually lead.

In a few minutes we were in Kiryat Moshe—home of Angel's Bakery and Mercaz HaRav—one of the centers of religious

Zionism. The street was cordoned off with police tape starting down at the bakery, about half a mile away from the yeshivah. I slowed to talk to the policeman there. "My son is missing. He studies at the yeshivah." He lifted the tape for me to drive under and told me to park up ahead, across from the yeshivah on the corner of Me'iri Boulevard—best known for its two kiosks which feed the neighborhood's hundreds of hungry yeshivah students.

When we got out of the car, we were greeted with the controlled chaos of a crime scene. The yeshivah is located on a wide four-lane street with a high fence running down the middle to keep pedestrians from crossing at any place other than the crosswalks. On the side of the street that is farther from the yeshivah, held back by the fence, were what looked like a hundred or so mostly black-hatted haredi demonstrators, massed together and making a good deal of noise. Across the fence, the section of the street closer to the yeshivah was filled with another multitude. There were dozens of police officers, army personnel, ambulance corps, and sundry officials. Some wore reflective vests, some were in fatigues, some in police uniforms. Everybody was in motion, moving somewhere, doing something—although the entire area of activity comprised only a narrow block-and-a-half. I went up to the first policeman I found and said that my son was missing. He directed me to the *hapak*—a Hebrew acronym for front-line command center—somewhere up ahead.

Wandering about among the crowd was like being at a surreal carnival. There was plenty of bright emergency lighting illuminating the street along with flashing blue and red strobes from the ambulances and police cars. I tried to find somebody who looked like he might be in charge—someone with some hardware on his epaulets. I spoke to an anonymous officer who told us to wait here, he would see what he could find out and return in a minute. In the meantime, we listened to the shouting crowd on the far side of the fence, and watched the activity all around us. I've lived in Israel long enough to know what a Middle Eastern promise of "just one minute" can mean, so after waiting a few, my son and I began to wander around again.

Now we met up with the first of a literal army of volunteers in reflective yellow vests who were floating about the scene—social workers. These were mostly middle-aged women, pulled out of bed in the middle of the night to administer what could best be described as a form of psychological first-aid. The first one we met, with her reading glasses held on by a string around her neck, seemed to be looking, like a boy scout, for someone to help cross the street. She noticed us, clearly marked as civilians by our lack of either uniforms or vests, wandering about and saw her chance. "Can I help you?" she implored. I told her my son's name. She shuttled off, clipboard in hand, promising to see what she could do. We continued to wander about. Another social worker spoke with us—this time within earshot of yet another—who, at the sound of "Avraham David Moses," snapped her head around like a dog hearing his name called. She told us to follow her.

We were led around the side of the Mercaz HaRav compound to Yashlatz's small entranceway, sandwiched between its diminutive one-basket basketball court and the even smaller yard fronting its dorm building. There I met Yehudit face-to-face for the first time. She was the high school's social worker. We had spoken several times by phone over the year about Avraham David. She had been meeting with him, attempting to get him back into the school's regular schedule ever since he had decided to spend nearly 18 hours a day studying only religious subjects on his own, skipping all of his classes. With her was Yashlatz' administrator, Avigdor, and one or two Jerusalem city officials. The two social workers conferred for a moment.

"We need a place to sit," Yehudit said. It wasn't clear what we needed to sit for, but I was relieved that these people seemed to know more than we did. In search of "a place to sit" we started in the direction of the dorm, entered the hallway, and then Yehudit changed her mind and we returned to where we had started. My son and I exchanged looks, both of us thinking, "not another run around." Avigdor reappeared with a set of keys and led us back toward the main road. He unlocked a gate in the fence surrounding Yashlatz and brought us to a double door at the top of some steps. The doors opened into a stairwell. At the top, straight ahead and a half-flight up was the *beit midrash*— the study hall. Next to it, on our right, was the Rosh Yeshivah's small office.

There, as we came to the top of the half-flight of steps, was Rabbi Yerahmiel Weiss, emerging from the *beit midrash*. He suddenly grabbed me in a hug and said, "The Lord gives, the Lord takes away." Now we knew. My son was gone—taken away in this latest murderous attack on Jews.

CHAPTER TWO:
A MARTYR'S FUNERAL

Oh, where have you been, my blue-eyed son?

BOB DYLAN, "A HARD RAIN'S A-GONNA FALL"

According to Jewish law, official mourning begins only after
the burial service is completed. My son was murdered on
Thursday evening at 8:30 pm. I arrived at Yashlatz a bit after
midnight – the first parent to do so. The funeral began Friday
morning at 10:00 am and ended at close to 2:00 pm. Before sitting
down on a wooden bench at the Kfar Etzion cemetery to remove my
leather shoes and begin the week of mourning, however, I would
talk dozens of times with my wife at home, call my family in the
US, be swabbed for DNA by the police, tell off an intrusive social
worker, come close to blows with the police about getting a burial
certificate, drive home, sleep in my clothes for an hour, make more
phone calls, travel back to Jerusalem to attend the mass funeral for
the eight murdered youths at Mercaz HaRav, return to my Efrat
synagogue where the funeral for my son continued, and then move
on to the nearby cemetery of Kfar Etzion. There, after watching
my son's body be lowered into the dark earth beneath the shade of

pine trees, I finally sat down and exchanged the leather clogs I was wearing for a cheap pair of imitation Crocs. The mourning period for my son had officially begun.

My son did not die alone. Huddled together with his friends in the library stacks, he was one of eight innocents murdered that night. This fact linked his death to something larger than his own privately-lived young life. However, the massacre of these eight youths, caught chatting with friends or studying Torah, was linked to something broader still. They died in a carefully planned terror attack aimed at slaughtering innocent Jews in Israel's capital city, Israel's reinvigorated *axis mundi*, Jerusalem. Another violent outburst aimed at somehow erasing the blemish of a Jewish presence in *dar al-Islam*, the Muslim-centric vision of the Middle East. For better or worse, this heinous bloodletting was not just a bit of random violence. Elishav Avihayil, Segev's father, would say, connecting their deaths to the ancient Temple service, "Our children were public sacrifices."

On the Friday morning of the funeral, my family and I were shepherded from our house (which had begun to feel like some sort of train depot with dozens of people flowing in and out) to Mercaz HaRav by another group of (this time local) social workers and a security detail. The latter was needed to enter the closed-off Kiryat Moshe neighborhood. At some point, between two and three o'clock the previous morning, Rabbi Weiss had approached us as we sat crowded in his small office to pitch the idea that the eight funerals would all start from Mercaz HaRav. As he shuttled between the families, I noticed that this idea to first hold a central ceremony, before each family took its dead son to his final resting place, morphed from a reasonable suggestion into "the families' request."

When we arrived at the yeshivah for the funeral on Friday morning, we were ushered into the plaza in front of the library. Unlike the night before, it was now filled with chairs for the families of the murdered students and its stone walls were covered with poster-sized death notices. There we sat, with barely three hours of sleep between my son, my wife and me. Also with us were my then first-grade daughter and her long term babysitter cum surrogate grandmother. We waited under the warm sun for the other families, who lived further from Jerusalem, to arrive. We waited for the bodies of our children to be carried in on stretchers by the respective *hevrot kadisha* (burial societies) who were responsible for ensuring their proper burial. We waited, perspiring, as the day grew hotter and thousands upon thousands crowded the street below the yeshivah and loudspeakers pleaded with them to let the "families of the martyrs" through. I was now the father of a martyr – one had who died a sacred death—killed not by mere accident, but sought out in a holy place of Torah learning and executed by a Moslem terrorist, who was intent on reaching his own private heaven via the ever-popular path of slaughtering Jews.

Bottles of water. If anyone profits from public funerals in Israel, it is the bottled water industry. As we sat and waited, boxes and boxes of bottled water made their way through the crowded mass of family, rabbis and politicians to be distributed among us. We were continually exhorted by the ever-hovering social workers to drink. "Do you want more water? Drink. Here, have some water." As we slowly baked in the sun, we downed bottle after bottle. Sitting and waiting, we drank and watched as other parents, grandparents, brothers, sisters, aunts and uncles of the eight murdered youths made their way, pushing through the crowds, to the packed plaza in the sun.

After half an hour or so, the bodies of our children began to arrive from wherever they had been kept for the few hours since they had been identified. Eight pairs of high-backed wooden benches taken from the study hall had been set up in front of us on the plaza. The benches in each pair faced each other, forming a sort of bed, and each bed held a sign marked with the name of one murdered student. These were the benches on which the murdered boys had sat for countless hours poring over their books. Now the benches would, for one last time, support their now-cold bodies. Each body was carried through the crowds on a stretcher, wrapped in a *tallit* (prayer shawl). The outlines of each young body could be made out through the woolen fabric in which they were swaddled. As each body was brought forward, his name was announced. With each name another cry went up from the crowd—something akin to a collective wave of pain.

As each name was called, I sat watching the reactions of the hundred yeshiva students who stood opposite me, on the path leading to the library, the boys who just yesterday had been my son's schoolmates. Fifteen- and sixteen-year-olds, teenagers who one would expect to find laughing over a pick-up game of basketball, howled as tears ran down their still downy cheeks. They cried for their dead friends. They cried at the sheer horror of death that had muscled in on their young lives.

This is what struck me more than anything. These adolescents should have been learning, playing, joking—all with the enviable, boisterous energy of teenage boys. Instead, they were standing in the hot sun, hanging on to each other to keep from collapsing, bawling with unfiltered grief. Each name, each body, was like the stab of a knife tearing another howl from these boys' throats. I sat across from where they stood, the eight still bodies laid out between us, holding my bottled water in the sun and quietly cried my own small tears. For them as much as for my own son.

Now it was time for the eulogies to begin. Time for the learned rabbis to speak. There were tears, comparisons to atrocities past, exhortations to be strong, to learn Torah. I found it difficult to follow. I kept looking at the bodies of my son and his fellow cadavers. But throughout it all, we family members sat passively, waiting in the sun until they finished. Then it was time for the eight fathers to stand and say *kaddish* (the mourner's prayer) for their sons.

Announcements were made over the loudspeakers, giving the details of where each boy was to be buried and where the buses which would transport people to the various burials were waiting. We waded out into the crush of the crowd, following Avraham David's stretcher-supported corpse. Here and there was a face I recognized. Those faces were connected to hands that reached out of the swarming mass to give a pat on the shoulder, a fleeting touch, trying to connect with us above the crowd's enveloping white noise even as we were swept forward by the sheer mass's strong current.

My six-year-old daughter was spent. She was hot, she was tired, and she had had enough of sitting and listening to adult speeches while staring at the human-shaped package wrapped in a *tallit* that she knew was her brother. Elisha Dan and I entered the ambulance with the body and my wife Leah got into a van filled with social workers to drop our daughter off at home before we continued with the next part of the funeral. My ex-wife, Rivkah, and her family were somewhere in the crowd, making their way back to Efrat.

Elisha Dan and I sat with the corpse in the cool of the ambulance.

Now it was just the three of us—finally out of the sun, away from the crowd. Elisha Dan and I talked about what we had been through so far and discussed the rest of the day still ahead of us. We had recently reviewed, as part of his schoolwork, a well-known Talmudic story about Rabbi Elazar ben Azariah's appointment to the head of the Sanhedrin, the High Court of the Second Temple era. Rav Elazar, although still a young man, was chosen to replace Rabban Gamliel, an established leader who had just been impeached. Rav Elazar, aware of the political-religious intrigue which had just led to the senior rabbi's dismissal, was worried about assuming the mantle of leadership. He discussed his concerns with his wife, wondering if the position was worth the trouble, since he himself might very well be ousted and replaced, just as his more powerful and politically savvy predecessor had been. His wife, the Talmud relates, asked whether one who owns a delicate glass vessel should never use it, out of fear that it might break. Her point made, Rav Elazar agreed to accept the appointment as head of the Sanhedrin. For me and my son this parable of the *cosa demokra*, the fragile glass, stood for the fragility of life itself. One cannot live up on the shelf, out of danger's reach, forever. That is not a life at all. Being in the world exposes our fragility. When it came my turn to speak at the funeral, I would mention this story. But, I would add (stressing the difference between the Hebrew active and passive tenses) that my son did not break—he had been broken.

Sitting in the ambulance with my two sons (one alive, one not), we made our way back to Efrat. I live right across the street from my synagogue. Outside, a crowd of hundreds had been waiting in the heat for us to arrive. My sons and I pulled up. Elisha Dan and I emerged first, then the *hevrah kadisha* pulled out Avraham David's shrouded body on a wheeled trolley which they brought to the synagogue's small courtyard. As Elisha Dan's friends, let out of school to attend the funeral, saw him, he fell into their arms. Finally, he too let loose the torrent of tears that he had been holding inside since late the previous night.

Seated in one of the plastic chairs that had been set up in front of the synagogue was my rabbi and friend, Menahem Froman. People crowded the stairs leading to the upper floor's patio and the small, sloping grassy hill across from the building was full of neighbors and friends. We waited for the Moriahs, my ex-wife's family, to arrive and then for my wife Leah, whose ride had been stopped again and again by the dozens of volunteer police charged with keeping traffic off our small town's streets while the funeral took place. There is a limit to anyone's patience—even in the most sober of circumstances. After waiting nearly an hour under the hot sun, our neighbors (and the head of the local *hevrah kadisha*) seemed to have reached theirs. I was urged, even though my wife was still trying to settle in our exhausted six-year-old daughter at home across the street, to get things going.

"People have been waiting for an hour already."

"Well, we can't start without my wife."

We compromised, and the rabbi began to recite psalms with the crowd—a stalling tactic which bought us the few minutes needed for my wife to find her place in one of the plastic chairs.

A traditional Jewish funeral consists of several distinct phases which move the mourners along the time-worn path of separation from the deceased. Much has been written about the liminality— that sense of being on the cusp—that death brings to those who mourn. Anyone ever exposed to Sociology 101 has heard of the ways that ritual is designed to help us step back from the precipice and move on to firmer ground. These discussions, whether sociological or psychological, are, for the most part, grounded in metaphors of space—of moving from one place to another, of being on the edge, stuck betwixt and between. But space and place are more than metaphor. While a funeral is liturgy and eulogy, it is also a dance around the actual physical placement of death among the living.

Here in Efrat, we, the family, are seated under the overhanging entrance to the synagogue. Directly in front of us lies the body, wrapped tightly in the *tallit* on the gurney in the sun. Across from us, facing us and the gurney, standing in the sun, are the hundreds of mourners who have come to accompany—the Hebrew term for funeral, *levayah*, means just this—both us and Avraham David. With the deceased at the center of attention, eulogies are spoken. It is customary, if somewhat unnerving for the uninitiated, to speak not only of the deceased, but directly to him. Children address their parents, brothers their siblings and in our case, parents their children.

After eulogizing the dead, and reciting the *kaddish* prayer, more movement occurs. The body is placed back in the ambulance, to be brought to the cemetery at the head of a procession. We follow on foot. Psalms are recited over a megaphone. Then, after a few yards and the completion of a psalm, we stand in place and I recite another *kaddish* for my son. This, in accordance with local custom, happens four times. Walking, standing, *kaddish*.

We walk down the long street on which we live. Now, instead of feeling like flotsam in a huge, unfamiliar river, I make my way slowly down my own street, surrounded by those I know—neighbors and friends. Every few minutes another friend comes up to me. We stop and hug, embracing each other with an intensity reserved for those times that emotion is so strong it needs be made physical, uncontainable within our bodies' confines. Here is Israel, here is Moshe, here is Baruch. I see those walking solemnly, those crying uncontrollably. And so we wend our way slowly down the street.

At some point I reenter the ambulance. We leave Efrat and drive to the cemetery. People get into their cars and follow us. At each junction we pass, a few dozen people stand clustered together, awaiting our arrival. As we drive by, they stand silently looking at the slowly moving line of vehicles on its way to the cemetery. These are people who didn't make the trip to Jerusalem or attend the service in Efrat. Instead, they stood waiting on the corners of their own villages—waiting outside for us to pass—so that they too could take part in the *levayah*. As we pass each group, driving slowly by, I can see the sobriety of their expressions. They stand in silent acknowledgement of death as it makes its way down the road to the local cemetery. Something about this, something, I think having to do with honor—with honoring the dead—is very moving for me. I turn as we pass each group, feeling that I should salute or something. But we are inside the ambulance and they can't see me.

Our local cemetery is beautiful. On the edge of the first town reestablished on the newly liberated lands of 1967, Kibbutz Kfar Etzion, it is verdant and well-cared for, birds sing overhead; it is just lovely. The kibbutz, built on land purchased by a group of Jews in the 1920s, lost its last stand in 1948 as attacking Arab irregulars and Jordanian soldiers killed the men left behind to defend Gush Etzion—the southern flank of Jerusalem. It was the children of Kfar Etzion, all brought up fatherless, who came back 20 years later to rebuild it and, I imagine, to mend their own broken hearts.

The graves lie in green-grassed terraces on a steep hill surrounded by tall pines. In the shade of the trees it is cool and quiet. A narrow curving path leads down from the parking lot to stone steps, which then lead down to the terrace where we will lay my son. Below that, on a slope which continues down into the valley, are tall, slender pine trees. They silently watch over the graves.

As I arrive at the freshly dug grave, I see the long package that is Avraham David lifted from the gurney and watch one of my neighbors, standing up to his chest in the earth, carefully begin to lower the body. The *tallit* is removed. The thick white plastic body bag is slit open. Inside this covering, he has been wrapped in white linen cloth. He is not heavy. At about 5'7", he probably weighs less than a hundred pounds. Another *kaddish*. Dirt begins to refill the hole, as those crowding around us each take a turn with one of the shovels stuck in the light-brown pile of earth. The funeral ends with the *hevrah kadisha* rabbi turning one last time to my son. The rabbi asks Avraham David's forgiveness if they haven't cared for him properly and implores Avraham David to be a heavenly advocate for the Jewish people.

Slowly, we turn from the grave and begin to walk back the way we came. On a rough-hewn wooden bench I pause to remove my leather clogs. My rabbi hands me my Crocs and takes my shoes. On the curving path leading up to the kibbutz road, two lines of people form. Now, the comforting of the mourners begins. Up and up I make my way between the hundreds who line the narrow road on either side. As I walk by, they all speak the same refrain, one after the other—"May you be comforted among the mourners of Zion and Jerusalem". It is like making one's way through a close forest of whispering trees. And as I pass by, they fall in, from either side, behind me. The rows collapse behind us, like a long zipper being pulled shut, into a long column, with us, the mourners, at its head. Up we walk. In the shade of the tall pines we all move in an organic choreography which brings the funeral proper to an end.

Places have changed. From accompanying the dead, from trailing after the body, the crowd now becomes a human chain following us, the mourners. The center has shifted—from the dead to the living.

The Jewish tradition is that mourners remain at home for the week of *shivah*. They sit on low stools and the world comes to them. The home even functions as a public synagogue. The three daily prayer services are held within—so that the mourner does not have to leave his home even to attend public worship. He is encased by visitors; surrounded by the walls of his home and by those who enter night and day. As the deceased was shrouded and lowered into the earth, the mourner, wearing the same torn clothing throughout the week, is enveloped by those who come to call. He is entombed for the week within the four walls of his home, surrounded by constant company, becoming the focus of the community and, in my case, a good chunk of the Jewish world. It is only in the few moments before falling asleep late each night, lying in the dark on my bed, that something opens up, the walls fall away and I cry—the tears running freely down my face as I sob into my pillow—at last alone in the dark, finally accompanied only by memory.

CHAPTER THREE:
A CONCISE FIELD GUIDE TO
CONDOLENCE CALLERS

If I knew for a certainty that a man was coming to my house
with the conscious design of doing me good,
I should run for my life....

HENRY DAVID THOREAU, *WALDEN, OR, LIFE IN THE WOODS*

Entire books have been written concerning shivah— the traditional seven day period of Jewish mourning. Some are punctilious compilations of its rules and regulations. Others discuss the deeper meanings behind the relevant customs— offering explanatory solace. This chapter is a guide of another sort. It is compiled out of my personal experience and is certainly not meant to replace other works of the same genus.

1. The Public Figure

The public figure is usually found at any gathering where he feels that his presence may help him to further his paramount goal of keeping himself in the public eye.

1a. The Elected Official.

This visitor to the house of mourning engages in an endless string of hobnobbing with those whose support he needs to keep him afloat in the style to which he has grown accustomed. He makes the rounds of weddings, circumcisions, and sundry family gatherings. He also makes *shivah* calls in cases of newsworthy deaths. In Israel, the presence of government ministers is usually heralded by the arrival of security personnel—tough-looking young men wearing blazers accessorized with a small earpiece, its wire curling curiously down into their jackets. They stand in the *shivah* home casting suspicious looks at anyone entering while their charge is in attendance, thus adding to the already surreal atmosphere. A minister may also be followed by an entourage pitching their favorite project to him—feeling that there's no better time or place to unfurl maps and building plans than in the already over-crowded living room of the mourner.

The mourner may take advantage of the minister's presence to query him on the issues of the day and thus distract himself from the business of grieving over his loss. Depending on the particular ministry represented, the mourner may discuss economics, foreign affairs or domestic politics. The mourner can be assured that no matter what the actual stance of the minister, he will be at pains to temper any disagreement with the mourner's own personal opinion so as not to offend. This makes for much more pleasant dialogue than the usual shouting-match style of Israeli politics.

1b. The Public Rabbi

In Israel, municipal rabbis are life-long government appointees. They may or may not function as what much of the Jewish world recognizes as a pulpit rabbi, instead doing the paper work needed to keep state-sponsored religion moving along. As religious figures, though, they often feel that their presence adds a certain gravitas to public events and so find it difficult to stay away from even semi-public gatherings like *shivah* homes. Certain rabbinic figures may have their loyal retinue (or at least their driver) announce their entrance to the assembled, so as to add to the general drama of the visit.

If one misses the dramatic entrance, this visitor may still be identified by the tedious monologue he aims at his captive audience. He usually offers the ad hoc congregation some dusty pearl of sagacity drawn from his long life of public service, often recalling in his heart how well the very same speech went over in the cold winter of 1958. He may often warm to his task as he drones on—his rising oratory silencing all other conversation. Although he knows neither the mourner nor the deceased, he does know the worth of his own wisdom and is more than gracious in sharing it with those assembled in their time of suffering.

The mourner may use the time taken by the delivery of a well-worn sermon to surreptitiously peruse some of the newspaper articles lying on the side-table, attempt to follow the faint wisps of conversation coming from those who luckily escaped to the kitchen just in time, or to amuse himself by marveling at how the speaker manages to enunciate so well despite the ill-fit of his dentures. The visit usually concludes with a limp but warm two-handed handshake offered by the visitor only after he is satisfied that his oratory has indeed hit the mark.

In order to encourage the segue from speech to leave-taking, the mourner should soberly nod his head and sigh upon the conclusion of the former, as if his visitor had succeeded in drawing apart the curtains covering one of life's eternal mysteries and the profundity of it all was nearly overwhelming. This helps induce the guest's departure as he feels that he must give his listeners space to digest the weight of his words.

2. The Talker

This visitor just can't help him or herself. It may be the quiet in the house of mourning that makes him uncomfortable—he feels obliged to fill up the dead space with his own voice. Unlike the public speaker, he is not as interested in talking to the crowd as he is in talking to someone, whether the actual mourner or just another guest. Regardless, he will go on and on, bouncing from subject to subject, willing to talk about anything so long as it keeps the silence at bay. He is more than happy to take his leave once the baton of noise-making has been passed to another.

3. The Flyer

This stranger, especially in casual Israel, may often be recognized by his too-formal dress. He has flown in from overseas at no little expense to make this *shivah* call and will not be shy about divulging to those sitting nearby the travails he underwent to make it to Israel. This may be preceded by the stock phrase: "When I heard, I just *had* to come." He knows neither the mourner nor the deceased, but following events in the media overseas just won't do it for him—he has to be there and see for himself. (Upon his return, he will be uniquely able to describe *everything* to those he left behind.)

The Flyer is, of course, the visitor with whom the mourner gets to play Jewish geography. In the Jewish world, six degrees of separation is unheard of—you can usually get a hit in three, if not sooner.

48

4. The Donor

This visitor has much in common with the previous type and it can be difficult to distinguish between them. The Donor, though, responds to tragedy with his bank account. Just as the Talker cannot abide the silence in the *shivah* home, the Donor cannot abide the lack of a project in memory of the deceased—in support of which he is earnestly interested in providing funds. Now, since the death of the mourner's loved one took place less than a week ago, the mourner may not have had time to think about a befitting memorial quite yet. No matter, the Donor will keep in contact in order to find out to whom or what he can contribute. He may even help the mourner by deciding that he is going to arrange for a gala something or other in the near future. This may be quite an expensive undertaking. No matter if the mourner himself may not actually be interested in such a grand event—it would look just terrible not to at least participate in this event undertaken in memory of one's own loved one. Luckily, it will take place sometime down the road, not right now.

6. The Student(s)

This visitor usually arrives as part of a group. The entire bunch has most likely been brought by their teacher or rabbi. They have come as part of their educational experience, probably their gap-year-in-Israel program. Their leader has spoken to them of tragedy in the abstract and now they have a chance to see it close up. This is their opportunity to observe firsthand the "courage in the face of death" displayed by the mourners.

They will probably not speak with the mourner. They are still not yet mature enough to fully participate, and will be content to uncomfortably observe the proceedings, stare at their shoes and try to keep from giggling nervously. Coming as they do in a bunch, they take up quite a bit of space in an already over-crowded home. But, they do not intend to stay long and spend most of their time keeping quiet so as not to miss the cue from their leader that they can leave already. However, having been instructed by this same group leader in the Laws of Comforting Mourners, they will all take pains to stand before the mourner, one after the other, and mumble out the traditional parting phrase of consolation, "May God comfort you amongst the mourners of Zion and Jerusalem." The more conscientious will have practiced saying this tricky Hebrew phrase and will get it out nearly painlessly. Others in the group, though, will stumble a bit, and need to repeat themselves, thus holding up the entire long line of teenagers-with-hands-in-pockets staring at the floor.

The mourner may try to estimate where exactly the line ends, but must not break off his one-after-the-other-after-the-other acknowledgements, lest the entire process grind to a halt while the students pause and await the mourner's attention before continuing. Everything else must wait until the mourner has cleared the entire group.

6. The Interrupter

This visitor has done his homework. He knows, like the Student, what he needs to say before he can take leave of the mourner. Unfortunately, he has a busy schedule and so cannot wait until the mourner has finished the serious, quiet conversation he is holding with someone else. Therefore, he loudly clears his throat and pushes his way toward the mourner to loudly announce, "May God comfort you amongst the mourners of Zion and Jerusalem," no matter what else the mourner may be doing. He then takes his leave, satisfied with having fulfilled his duty as written in the great Codes of Jewish law.

7. The Colleague/Boss

This visitor may also fall into one of the other categories, but his distinguishing trait is his connection to the mourner's work. While a lucky few enjoy both their occupation and workplace, most people can easily identify their bosses and co-workers in any Dilbert comic. If the visitor is a colleague after one's job or an annoying boss, the mourner may make use of the temporary leverage offered by the moral high ground of victimhood to make *him* squirm for a change. This can be accomplished either by steadfastly ignoring the visitor or steering the conversation to points sure to make him uncomfortable. ("Death makes one appreciate one's *real* friends"; "Missing out on that promotion seems so insignificant now"; etc.) Care should be taken, however, for most likely the mourner will have to return to work sooner rather than later, unencumbered by any moral high ground.

8. The Contact Aggrandizer

This visitor has only the faintest of connections with the deceased, but especially if the deceased was well-known or his death newsworthy, he will milk it for all it is worth. The mourner may overhear, for example, something along the lines of, "Yes, my grandson and he were great friends in elementary school." This may have been true 25 years ago. It also may be that this grandson actually taunted and teased the deceased only a few years ago in grade school, and was anything but a friend. This guest is usually content to make a brief appearance aimed at relaying to others his own important connection to the tragedy. Whether the mourner should grin and bear it or point out that "Yes, I recall my son coming home in tears after being picked upon yet again by your lout of a relation" is a difficult call.

9. The Night-Owl

This caller leads a busy life but makes the effort to reach the mourner's home, even if it means arriving quite late. Yes, the chairs are being stacked, and the floor swept, but even if it is midnight and mourner would like nothing better than to get some rest, the night-owl will sit himself down to offer his condolences. As this nocturnal visitor arrives at a house empty of other callers, he often assumes that he must make an extra effort at consolation despite the hour. The mourner may find that letting nature take its course and allowing himself to drift off, chin to chest, is the only surefire way to end the day's activities.

10. The Helper

This visitor often goes unnoticed by the mourner himself during *shivah*. He, or more likely she, will arrange for food to be prepared for the family, deliver it, do the dishes quietly in the kitchen and even wash the floor while the mourner is napping, trying to gather strength for the next round of visitors. Depending upon the particular family structure, the Helper may also take it upon herself to entertain the mourner's children who have been short-changed of parental attention for the duration. In short, the Helper knows that the mourner and his family are on the verge of being crushed under the burden of loss. Even in the best of times, the stress of having to cope with the crowds who make their way into his home would be difficult, and the Helper does her best to keep things running as painlessly as possible.

It is quite appropriate to buy this visitor a gift in the days following the *shivah*, when the mourner finds out who it was that did all those little things that kept his home in one piece during the *shivah*. It is also quite appropriate to be inspired to become a helper oneself next time the need arises in the neighborhood.

11. The Davener

This visitor, almost always male, arrives, puts on his *tefillin* or takes out his *siddur* and does what he came to do—pray in the mourner's home. He may not linger or do anything else. This is his way of being there for the mourner. Without him, there may not be a *minyan* (the quorum necessary for recitation of the *kaddish*). He should know that his presence is appreciated.

12. The Friend of the Deceased

This visitor, although not an official mourner, is probably suffering from the mourner's loss, because it is also his. A part of his life has also been excised away. Commiseration—the sharing of mutually felt pain—can open something deep inside of both.

The deceased's friend can also tell the mourner much about the deceased—sometimes things that the mourner couldn't even imagine. While the mourner has his own memories, the stories told by this friend are precious. They add texture and color, allowing the mourner to reconstitute the life lost more clearly and more deeply than he could on his own. The mourner should record these tales. He will want to listen to them again.

13. The Friend

A true friend makes the unbearable somehow sufferable. He

knows when to talk and when to keep quiet. He offers the mourner space to be himself, without the need for any stiff upper lip. With a look, he can share the mourner's exasperation with some of the other visitors mentioned in this Guide. The mourner should know that in the future, when the rawness of loss has receded, both will laugh together when they look back at this week.

SEGURIDAD
EN LA
BICICLETA

Reglas De Carretera
Para Los Ciclistas

- ▶ Comunicarle a un adulto si algo esta roto o anda mal en tu bicicleta.
- ▶ Siempre usa el casco de seguridad.
- ▶ Viste con colores brillantes, así otros podrán verte mejor.
- ▶ Recuerda un asiento por ciclista.
- ▶ Mantén ambas manos en el manillar.
- ▶ Mira a la izquierda, derecha, izquierda hacia el transito en las señales de pare y caminos de entrada antes de montar en la carretera.
- ▶ Obedece las señales y semáforos de transito.
- ▶ Corre en el lado derecho de la carretera, en la misma dirección del flujo de transito de autos.
- ▶ Siempre usa señales de mano al detenerte o al virar.
- ▶ Mantente alerta al tráfico cercano a ti.
- ▶ Al montar con otros, corran en una sola hilera.

Señal Izquierda   Señal Derecha   Señal Pare

BIKE SAFETY

Tips for Safe Bicycle Riding

▶ Tell an adult if anything is broken or wrong with your bike.

▶ Always wear a bicycle safety helmet.

▶ Wear brightly colored clothing so that others can see you better.

▶ Remember: one seat = only one rider!

▶ Keep both hands on the handlebars.

▶ Look all ways for traffic at stop signs and driveways before riding out into the street.

▶ Obey traffic signs and lights.

▶ Ride on the right-hand side of the street in the same direction as the flow of automobile traffic.

▶ Always use hand signals when stopping or turning.

▶ Be aware of surrounding traffic.

▶ When riding with others, ride single file.

Signal Left   Signal Right   Signal Stop

www.AAA.com
ShareTheRoad.AAA.com

Stock#3154

CHAPTER FOUR:
WEEKEND EDITION

"Television is not the truth, television
is a goddamn amusement park."

FROM THE FILM *NETWORK*, WRITTEN BY PADDY CHAYEFSKY

It is Friday night. A few hours have passed since we buried my son. My wife, my daughters and I are joined for the Sabbath by Rabbi Menahem Froman and his wife, Hadassah. They are, simply put, holy people. In their presence, on the holy Sabbath, mourning is replaced with something less painful, something closer to God.

Our house has been cleaned and yesterday's dishes washed by a friend's 18-year-old daughter. Food for the day's three meals has been prepared for us by our neighbors. We sit around our Sabbath table on our day of rest, no phone or television allowed to disturb us. At the same time, tens of thousands of Israeli families—many of them traditionalists who have been to synagogue and made *kiddush* themselves but do not necessarily "keep the Sabbath" completely—sit down to watch the evening news. No matter which channel they choose to view, they will be treated to in-depth coverage of the week's top story—the Mercaz HaRav attack.

The Israeli government long ago gave up its television monopoly. Now three local channels offer viewers nearly round-the-clock news coverage. With competition came the end of stodgy men in glasses reading the news. All the stations have kept up with the times and brought in younger and much more attractive anchors since commercial broadcasting was introduced. I'm sure that any of them could find work as a fashion model should reading the news grow old. And like everywhere else, "the news" is as much about interpreting events as it is about reporting them.

Let me start with Channel Two—the most popular news station. The anchor of the Channel Two weekend news report, *Friday Studio*, is Yair Lapid, a well-known media "personality" who used to host a talk show and made the move to more serious newscasting mid-career. The program contained filmed segments detailing the attack and its victims' funerals in all-too-graphic detail. These were interspersed with Lapid and his crew of four commentators cross-talking in typical Israeli fashion as they debated the implications of the attack.

The TV analysts emphasized the frustrations that a "lone terrorist" presented to the security forces. Abu Dheim was a worst-nightmare scenario—unpredictable, acting alone, and in possession of an Israeli ID card that allowed him to move freely throughout the country. There was much made of the particular gruesomeness of these boys' deaths—they played the recording of a student's cell phone call for help, during which shots could be heard, and showed picture after picture of the carnage. Lapid commented that the "war on terror" was fought in the media as much as anywhere else: it was the Israeli government itself which had sent a photographer to capture the horrible scenes they showed their viewers. The powers-that-be wanted to show the world what suffering under Arab terror looked like: so much blood that it lay in actual pools, religious garments stained as if they had been dipped in red paint and eight body bags, all lined up in a row. When the news crew aired reactions from around the world, Lapid wondered aloud how Bernard Kouchner, the (Jewish) French Foreign Minister, could have so coldly dismissed this attack as just another round of continuing Middle Eastern violence. "We might have expected a bit more sympathy," Lapid commented.

Channel One is the public station. It broadcast an extra-long special edition devoted mostly to the attack. Their news program offered the most in-depth coverage of the attack, exploring it from a variety of angles. It makes for fascinating viewing, as worthy of close reading as any other cultural commentary.

The thirty-something veteran anchorwoman Geula Even began her career as a short-haired, eyeglass-wearing, librarian-like young woman. She has morphed into a stunner with stylishly severe, straight jet-black hair that runs down her back and is cropped over her eyes into harsh right-angle bangs. When the news begins, she comes into view sitting behind a long modernist glass counter.

> It's nearly always like this in our country – but this has been one of the more difficult weeks to digest in recent times – 2 soldiers killed in Gaza, a tracker killed by an IED [improvised explosive device] on the security fence, Kassam and Grad missiles being effortlessly launched and the horrendous attack yesterday on the yeshivah in Jerusalem in which eight students were murdered.

Scenes of the attack, the funerals, sound bytes from the boys' friends, snippets of eulogies, statements from the police: these give a picture of what happened the previous night. Over the course of the hour-plus broadcast, Even will try to place the attack into the wider context of Israel's struggle with the Hamas in Gaza. She will interview the station's expert correspondents. She will talk to politicians from the Left and the Right. Her overarching theme will be the connection of this massacre with the IDF's actions the previous week in Gaza.

In brief, between February 27th and March 2nd the IDF had conducted a series of strikes against the Hamas-led Gazan terrorist infrastructure. The army wanted to end the rain of missiles on Israel's southwest flank. The assault had begun shortly after the Hamas military coup in the summer of 2007. By the end of February it seemed that the government had decided it was time to put a stop to it. But over a long weekend of IDF sorties and intrusions, it also seemed that the sh-t had hit the fan.

180 rockets were launched by Hamas at progressively more distant and larger Israeli population centers, public bomb shelters were ordered open in Ashkelon and the IDF succeeded in destroying just one of Hamas' major arms caches containing hundreds more missiles. Israeli forces also struck at those transporting, launching, aiding and abetting the general rain of terror against Israel's cities. Over a hundred Palestinians were killed. Of course, depending upon who you asked, you would be told either that there were some unfortunate collateral deaths of civilians (around 10% of all deaths) due to Hamas terrorists' use of civilian cover, or that Israel was wantonly targeting innocent civilians in its attempt at perpetuating a holocaust against the Palestinian people. Things hadn't looked so grim since the Israeli withdrawal from Gaza in 2005.

Geula Even and her panel of experts talked about the Arab rage in the streets, of how the Mercaz HaRav attack was the bitter fruit of IDF operations; payback for Baruch Goldstein's Hebron massacre years before (which had recently been reenacted on Hamas TV); Iranian-sponsored remote control terror. A short visit to Abu Dheim's Jabel Mukhaber neighborhood by the station's "territories" correspondent was aired. It featured an older Arab man, wearing a traditional *keffiah*, being interviewed in Arabic:

Q: What do you think of the attack?

A: What do you think about what happened to the children in Gaza? The houses that are destroyed above the children's heads? That's my opinion.

A later segment opened with scenes of the flags of the PLO, Hamas, and (the voice-over told viewers) "even Hezbollah" hanging over the terrorist's house. Viewers were then dramatically informed that "we are not talking about Gaza or the West Bank, but East Jerusalem." The piece ended with the reporter concluding: "There is one thing that everybody agrees upon— yesterday's attack was a response to Israel's actions in Gaza—that is what they say here."

Tit for tat, an eye for an eye—the *logic* of revenge makes sense. It also offers, in some perverse way, hope. For if there is logic behind the terror, then somewhere there is a logical solution to be found. But even while trying to fit this attack into the larger framework of the ongoing Israel-Arab conflict, to make sense of it through contextualization, Geula Even couldn't help pointing out something else, something more viscerally disturbing about the death of these boys.

The attack in Mercaz HaRav has shaken the Israeli public, something that tens, if not hundreds, of Kassam

*and Grad missiles that land on the southern townships,
has not. It is not pleasant to admit, as we are not those
who experience this day after day, but it seems that we
have gotten used to this [shelling in the south]. It sounds
terrible, but for most of us, this is already routine. But
the terror attack in Jerusalem in which eight youths
were murdered for no reason, again raises the tension
level and returns us to the days of horrible terror which
we very much wanted to put behind us.*

For all the attempts at making sense, at finding some cause which
could explain to us why, Even still cannot stop herself from telling
us that these youths "were murdered for *no reason*." Despite their
best efforts at cause and effect, even the dispassionate experts
know that nothing explains the scenes broadcast this evening: the
streams of blood that ran down the library floor, the bullet-ridden
holy books, the garments drenched red held up to the camera. And
the illogic of *no reason* brings only dread—dread that the days
when pizza shop patrons were being blown to pieces were back.
Dread that the killing won't end. Dread that the dangerous dance
between Arab and Jew is not a dance at all—but a brutal fight in
which we could either kill or be killed. The false hopes and dreams
of Oslo's "new Middle East" and the difficult retreat from Gaza—
each accompanied by sugary visions of peace, *shalom, salaam*—
were crumbling, replaced once again by *tallit*-draped bodies being
lowered into the ground.

The most fascinating piece of coverage offered by public
television was a documentary short film, the likes of which one
would be hard pressed to find on another news program; not so
much news, as a video essay, a reflective contemplation on terror
in Israel shot by Channel One's resident documentary filmmaker,

Uri Goldstein. Like many documentary directors, Goldstein offers filmed social commentary. He accompanies his work with his own narration that ranges from the poetically complex to the simply interrogative. Weaving together a mixture of interviews, archival and made-to-order footage, Goldstein himself stays off camera. But his distinct, disembodied voice speaks to his viewers throughout—the voice of conscience, or perhaps, in his own mind, of something even higher.

The opening shot trails an MDA [Israeli Red Cross] motor-scooter gliding in the thin morning traffic towards Kiryat Moshe.

There is a moment when of necessity we clean up the traces of the past.

And the pictures of last night

[shot of a ZAKA volunteer holding up a bloody *tallit katan*]

are already cemented in our memory.

[shot of soon-to-become iconographic bullet holes in glass door].

Mercaz HaRav, this morning at seven.

[shot of mechanical street-sweeper machine and workers cleaning up refuse from last night's crowds]

With the passage of time, the experience will meld with the attacks of the past we store on file.

[shot of morning prayers in the yeshivah taken from below via the window into the Mercaz HaRav study hall].

The exceptions: the families of, and the witnesses to, the murdered and the wounded.

[shot of religious Jewish woman and children walking near the yeshivah]

And children whose viewpoint will be shaped: some towards revenge; some towards indifference.

[shot of Arab children in what appears to be an urban war zone]

Some towards despair; some towards hope—children from both sides.

In his sonorous voice-over to the accompanying pictures, some painfully graphic and some quite banal, Goldstein relates that the shadow of victimhood spills out well beyond those murdered the night before. While there were eight victims, many more were victimized—"children from both sides." Unfortunately many are captured by the past, its images forever engraved in their lives, trapped and traumatized by its grip. It matters little whether they are Jew or Arab.

The next act in Goldstein's piece consists of a "tour" of the scene. Haredi teenagers, already experts in the minutiae of the previous evening, act as guides and describe some of the attack's more fascinating details. Here the bullet holes, here the sacred text shot through, here the spot where an "officer named Shapiro" shot the terrorist. The banalization of the site, it seems, has begun. Already it is being turned into a must-see spot, complete with tour guides.

Suddenly, the scene changes. From the yeshivah, the viewer is transported somewhere else, it is not clear to where. A car is driving down a street. Suddenly, there are young Arab men hurling stones. They pelt the car at close range in the narrow street. The sound of rock on metal is frightening. The entire rear window shatters. There is a real viciousness to this attack captured on film. Unlike a lion taking down its prey in the savannah, here there is no poetry, only savageness. And as the scene unfolds, Goldstein's narration informs his viewers that they are watching a "near-lynching" that took place earlier in the week in East Jerusalem. (Those who had followed the news may have recalled that this was an attack on a hapless municipal inspector who barely escaped with his life.)

The chaos worries us. We need to mark a reason, where did it start.

On Salah A-Din St. in Jerusalem there was almost a lynching this week.

It reflected the rage of the Arabs over the deaths in Gaza.

From this archival footage, the scene segues into a shot of the same street, this time taken from inside a moving car. Only now, everything is quiet. No crowds, no noise. Soon we will make our way out of this urban setting into a more pastoral one. Soft contemporary Israeli music plays as the car follows a military jeep down the winding roads, and the camera records goats and sheep grazing on the surrounding hills.

The village of Jabel Mukhaber, seven a.m.

The parallel couldn't be clearer—from the scene at the yeshivah at seven in the morning we have made our way, via a storm of violence, to the "Arab side." Through the miracle of television, somehow time has stood still. It is still seven a.m. Here, Goldstein tells us, the residents fear for their livelihoods. They wonder whether they will be able to return to their jobs in "Jewish Jerusalem."

In an interior shot of a small grocery, Goldstein (always off camera) asks two thirty-something Arabs behind the counter the strangest of questions:

"Were you glad yesterday?"

"Let's say, when they kill people, you're not happy— no matter where. Also when you see things like this in Gaza, we're not happy. Also in this case we're not happy. But, [shrugging] these things happen."

I wonder what Goldstein expected in answer to his query. Was this shopkeeper going to reveal himself to be a supporter of mass murder while being filmed by an Israeli? Does he think that these Arabs are animals or idiots? Or does he suspect that his viewers are?

As Goldstein's camera continues its tour of Jabel Mukhaber there is a shot of some Arabic graffiti spray-painted on a wall. Goldstein's voice-over seems to be a translation of the writing. Something poetic-sounding about guns, and blood, and land which barely makes any sense. (When I send the frame to a friend of mine who is an intelligence officer specializing in Arabic he translates it completely differently: "No and a thousand no's to bargaining. Yes to the resistance for the sake of our martyrs' blood." I guess Goldstein thought that nobody would fact-check him.)

And now we leave the Arabs. Old black and white footage of a youth wearing a large knit *kippah* jumping off the roof of a police paddy-wagon and escaping arrest suddenly appears on the screen. In grainy archival footage we see small mobile homes parked in the desert and obviously religious Jews walking through the sands. Goldstein narrates:

*Twenty six years ago, Rabbi Tzvi Yehudah Kook died.
At the time, I was in Sinai. This is the rabbi who
turned religious Zionism from something moderate
into something fixated on the great feat: the hastening
of salvation through deeds. [It was he] who saw the
settling of Greater Israel as divine—and so pushed the
youth to more radical religiosity, to patriotism, and it
goes without saying, to more extreme nationalism.*

Now we hear another voice, that of a pontificating elderly man:

*This is not peace, this peace has no substance, this
peace is a false peace. True peace is that found written
in the Torah!*

We assume that this is the voice of this same rabbi, Rabbi Tzvi
Yehuda Kook, son of Israel's first Chief Rabbi and longtime
dean of the Mercaz HaRav yeshivah, named after his father.
Some viewers may know that the forced removal of the 3,000
Sinai settlers as part of the Israel-Egypt peace treaty occurred
in April 1982, twenty-six years before the Mercaz HaRav
massacre. Fewer probably know that Rav Tzvi Yehudah died a
month prior to the evacuation.

Now we return to Mercaz HaRav. Goldstein will tell us, in
a laconic tone that makes it sound nearly anti-heroic, of the
paratrooper officer who "did as he was required" and "stopped the
murderer." He will talk to a bystander who turns out to be the aunt
of Neriah Cohen, the youngest of the boys killed. She nervously
pulls at her cheek in grief as she tells him why she has come to
this mass funeral. We will be taken back to Shaare Zedek Medical
Center, to the emergency room entrance where an ambulance
driver is wiping down his vehicle as Goldstein asks:

Would the wounded care, in the moment of truth, whether
their ambulance was clean or dirty? Of course not, but
the driver does what he must, and that's OK. Maybe this
is his therapy after last night.

I ask myself, should we care that we are watching a private
ambulance, not one used for trauma victims, but for prearranged
transport of chronically ill outpatients? There is little chance that
the driver had anything to do with the attack's victims the previous
evening. This ambulance certainly did not. Is it OK that Goldstein
does what he must—use a shot that seems too good to pass up,
despite its irrelevance? Maybe this is his way of coping, of fitting
facts to his own thoughts.

Now come more horrific descriptions of the attack which we have
already heard during previous reports. Back to the terrorist's house,
where Goldstein gets his name wrong. No matter. No one in the
village will talk to him now. We watch a mourning tent for the dead
terrorist being hammered together.

They don't agree to talk or to brag, lest they also suffer.
They have been entangled with the Jews for forty years.

The implication is that the Arabs are scared of the consequences
of discussing their feelings. They, after all, are dependent upon the
Jews for their livelihood.

The next scene is set at a soccer field adjacent to Shaare Zedek
Medical Center. Goldstein interviews an off-duty, twenty-
something soldier who has come to watch his team practice there
before a big game. Goldstein asks the soldier for his reaction to the
attack and is told:

As a Jerusalemite, it hurts. As a Jew, it hurts, as a
soldier, it hurts. It simply hurts.

You saw it at home?

No, on base.

On TV?

Yes.

What was the atmosphere?

Disgusting. Useless security alerts. A disgusting feeling.

[shot of newspaper with banner headline "MASSACRE IN YESHIVAH"]

[shot of the soldier smiling, together with a friend who is in on the joke]...*I have a psychologist's permit to go to every Beitar* [a Jerusalem soccer club] *game.*

If not, what would happen to you?

If not, I start to go crazy—to flip over tables. ...

... Of course.

Terror may be painful, but soccer is soccer. Standing under the blue skies above the verdant playing field, Goldstein commiserates with the soldier's odd but understandable malady. Life goes on, doesn't it?

The film returns yet again to Mercaz HaRav as the names of the murdered are being called out at the end of the mass funeral. The crowds are being told where each will be buried; where public transportation is available to take them to each of the eight separate internments. Grieving youth, shots of bullet holes and the credits roll. Another work by Goldstein, the master, is complete.

After watching this film several times, I wonder what kind of an ass this Goldstein is. I can understand that in his rush to complete his work he may fuddle some Arabic, fudge an ambulance or a name. I can understand his liberal values wanting to focus on the "suffering on both sides" — it's ready-made news commentary. (Like a report in Britain's *The Telegraph* which claimed that even though Abu Dheim came from an "upper-middle class home," he "faced a future of employment in menial jobs." What?! He worked in *one* of his family's several businesses as a bus driver. The same work that plenty of my neighbors do. But, it sounds good—desperate man forced into terror….)

Goldstein's game, played while he safely hides behind the camera, is pathos. "Suffering is universal, isn't it?" the all-seeing, but never seen, disembodied prophet teaches us. But blame is not. And that is what he is after. He cannot abide, in his words, "the chaos." The Arab rage is understandable — the vicious, near-killing of a city employee reasonably "reflected the rage of the Arabs over the deaths in Gaza." So, Goldstein may feel that the slaughter in "Jewish Jerusalem" is understandable, if regrettable. He shows us a mere (mistranslated) glimpse of ideological graffiti, but the Arabs he talks to are not happy over any death — theirs or ours. Their livelihoods are at risk. Sad creatures, Goldstein's Arabs, and really through no fault of their own. They too mourn the loss of one of theirs. And for all the supposed linkage between Gaza and Jerusalem, not one reporter ever found a trace of actual evidence that Abu Dheim himself was motivated by this. No note, no recorded last will or testament. And no reporter took the time and effort to trace, let alone mention, the well documented visceral hatred of Jews preached by tens of local *imams* and taught to thousands of school children in Palestinian Authority approved textbooks. How many times does one need to hear about the evils of these descendents of "apes and swine" and about the rewards awaiting those who murder them before erupting into terrible violence?

But the Jews? Low-hanging fruit. If you seek fanaticism, that's where you'll find it. Although long departed, Rabbi Zvi Yehudah Kook is shown by Goldstein to be a fanatic who stole the soul of Zionism, who made it into something perverse, something at odds with everything noble. Under Rabbi Tzvi Yehudah's reign, a dark, radically nationalistic, messianic monster was born. That enemy of peace itself. We heard it in his own words.

Essentially, Goldstein's film asks, can you really blame the Arabs? See, they aren't dancing in the streets (not in Goldstein's film, at least). The eternal "cycle of violence" wearily continues. We should be thankful that most of us Jews can quickly move on to what is more important, to today's big soccer game, for example. We should get over it, get on with our lives, not get bogged down, not let fanaticism drag us down.

For Uri Goldstein there are plenty of victims, and victimhood is universal; there is no difference between Arab and Jewish. Sadness extends both to East and West Jerusalem. The real villain of the piece is not the terrorist who brutally slaughtered these youngsters, for he too is dead and being mourned by his family. It is not any of the Arab youth who the previous week, through no fault of their own, let the municipal inspector get away before they could finish off what they started. Now the streets are calm. No, Goldstein has met the enemy and it is—that fanatic old rabbi who forced his followers into the depravity of radical religious nationalism. Do we wonder what events of 26 years ago have to do with the deaths of these teenagers last night? The irony of the father's sins being visited upon the sons cannot be any clearer, can it? The students at Mercaz HaRav were obviously murdered on the very alter of fanaticism that their teacher himself built. He was the one who rejected peace. No wonder his students pay the price.

For anyone who follows Israeli culture this sentiment is not surprising. For years, many members of Israel's Left have treated the "settlements/occupation" as a black hole into which all of society's ills may be stuffed. If (and I am not making this up) a middle-aged Jewish bicyclist is killed by a hit-and-run Jewish teenage driver who has had a bit too much to drink, then, of course, a major newspaper editor will write that it's *really* the fault of the occupation which has so coarsened our society.

In 2003, a young man and an infant were killed in an Arab terrorist attack on a small settlement south of Hebron called Negohot. The attack took place on the first night of the Jewish New Year, in the home of a former student of mine, just as his family and another were sitting down to their holiday meal. Pictures of the scene featured in the press showed the once festively-set table in a shambles—mute testimony to celebration turned into tragedy. A prominent left-wing artist wrote to *Haaretz* (the most left-leaning Israeli daily) protesting that the inclusion of such pictures should not be permitted as they unnecessarily "humanized" the settlers. Better to only show the outside of their homes, preferably from an angle that illustrates how they intruded upon the Arab landscape.

Five years later, *Haaretz* continued not to disappoint its readership who expected to hear only the worst of the "settlers". They sent a reporter to speak to my ex-wife. I don't know how the conversation went or all of its actual content. What I do know is that at some point the conversation moved to the question of making "political use" of the murders. As I mentioned above, the Israeli government had sent a photographer to record the horrific scene of the attack in order to show the world a more visceral view of what Arab terrorism meant. The reporter asked Avraham David's mother what she thought of this. She felt that it was "legitimate."

Bingo! Despite the fact that most of the reported conversation focused on the pain of loss rather than on politics, the headline read: *Mother Of Mercaz HaRav Victim Backs "Political Use" Of Son's Murder.* In *Haaretz'* ideological worldview this was the story—the cynical exploitation of a son's death by a West Bank settler. (Of course, they evince the same disdain when Palestinian parents and institutions parade their dead or wounded before the world's media. Oh…they actually endorse that kind of politicization.)

I was also interviewed a number of times by the media. At the large gathering which took place at Yashlatz and Mercaz HaRav on the day the *shivah* period ended, I was asked to speak live to a reporter from Channel One. The reporter was a young religious man by the name of Arnon Meir. He described the atmosphere at the yeshivah and the events scheduled to take place. The anchor woman Keren Neubach, though, seemed more interested in what she described as a "call by some of the right-wing organizations" to which "some of the bereaved families were, maybe, a party to," to march on Abu Dheim's still-standing house and tear it down. This, she explained, was meant to be "a statement" by these groups that if the government wouldn't take action, then they would. She added that in actuality, the organizers of this "statement" had already decided against this plan of action. However, there were perhaps still "calls" of this nature being heard.

Meir patiently explained that there *was* a good deal of frustration among the general public and anger in the yeshivah over the fact that the Abu Dheim family had been permitted to erect a "mourning tent" and that the terrorist's house had not been slated for sealing or destruction as punishment for his crimes. A protest march was planned for next week, but certainly not one aimed at physically assaulting anyone or damaging any property. It was clear to Meir that even if that was the aim of a planned protest (which it wasn't), the police would certainly not let anyone near the Abu Dheim's residence.

Incredible as it may appear to anyone interested in objective reporting, Neubach was intent on following a story which she herself already knew was not going to happen. She *knew* that the anonymous right-wing organizations she had referred to as responsible had already recalled their support for this supposed "statement," but felt compelled to keep on looking for some thread of a story that would support her desire to report a violent confrontation between the "radical right" and the Arabs.

Meir, holding a microphone and relaying me questions from the studio, asked me how I felt, and to describe my murdered son. After a few sentences, though, the short interview turned to the subject in which his anchor was primarily interested—confrontation. She had heard rumors of a petition circulating among the bereaved families demanding that the then-Prime Minister, Ehud Olmert, take action against the Abu Dheims. He wanted to know whether the families had organized themselves, did we have plans to protest.

I was a bit taken aback by the question. All of the families had spent the previous week bunkered down in their own homes mourning. We barely knew each other, and certainly hadn't had time to meet or plan anything. But again, the story the news anchor was seeking had more to do with a pre-scripted sense of ongoing conflict between Jews and Arabs than with the particulars of this attack. Unfortunately for her, I couldn't satisfy the audience with the type of answer she was seeking. I told Meir that in the midst of my still-fresh mourning I hadn't found the time to be angry, that I hadn't seen a petition of any sort, and that my main feeling was one of shock at the presence of such horrendous evil made manifest by the attack which left eight innocent youths dead.

The worst case, though, of conflating content and imagined context was a "scoop" by veteran political correspondent Ayalah Hasson on Channel One. She reported that a group of young men with access to weapons (they were all IDF veterans with gun permits) had begun planning a revenge attack against an Arab target. According to her, they had met two days after the attack on Saturday night in Mercaz HaRav (this she repeatedly stressed) with two rabbis: one was someone who taught at the yeshivah itself, and the other was someone she depicted as a well-known radical rabbinic figure. The group had been discussing whether the IDF would respond to the attack on Yashlatz and Mercaz HaRav. Supposedly, one of the rabbis had told the group that if the IDF didn't act "then you respond."

According to Hasson, three of the young men then traveled to another rabbi seeking approval for a plan to attack an Arab "connected to the Temple Mount." This rabbi reportedly gave his blessing to their plan. Hasson claimed that the security forces knew of the plan and were on the alert. The evening's anchors worriedly speculated out loud whether there might be other plans afoot, unknown to the authorities.

This report spread quickly throughout the media, who eagerly fanned the flames of suspicion that a new Jewish underground was going to sprout up, one that would seek vengeance for the attack on Mercaz. It was discussed on well-listened-to radio programs and written up in the newspapers. It resonated with the other reports and commentary which cast Mercaz HaRav as a bastion

73

of the radical right. (One well-known commentator apologized in print after declaring it a "fascist institution." Well, sort of. He explained that he hadn't meant that the eight young victims were *themselves* fascists….)

The yeshivah and well-connected religious Zionist public personalities vigorously denied that any such meeting had taken place. The yeshivah complained to the Israeli Broadcasting Authority, asking for Hasson to be censured and threatened to sue for defamation. Religious MK Zevulun Orlev called for a police investigation of the allegations, feeling sure that the only evidence they would turn up was that this was another attempt at maligning the religious Zionist community.

Official response was quick to come. The Israel Broadcasting Authority spokesperson offered an almost talmudic response to Mercaz HaRav's complaint against Hasson's report. She had not actually claimed that a rabbi from Mercaz HaRav was *behind* the initiative. This much was true. They said she had emphasized that the meeting had "coincidentally occurred in the yeshivah with no connection to its rabbis or personalities." This claim was patently false. Hasson had, in fact, repeated the meeting's location twice— clearly implying that it was no coincidence at all – and stressed the fact that one of the rabbis present was from Mercaz HaRav.

Within two days, the General Security Service stated quite plainly that there was no basis to claims of any Jewish group seeking revenge. So much for Hasson's claim that the police were warily awaiting developments in this conspiratorial plot.

As these examples show, the Israeli media has difficulty keeping its ideological agenda from interfering with what should be objective reporting. Goldstein's own docu-drama is more of the same. Yet, its very pretentiousness made it even more difficult to stomach. The odd question that Goldstein put to the Arabs, "Were you glad yesterday?" makes more sense if understood against the background of his own loathing of Mercaz HaRav. (I wonder whether it reveals more about his own thoughts on the murder at Mercaz HaRav than he would care to admit on film.) Goldstein's work is "artistic"—hence it is not held to the same standards as "the news." It is crowned with a halo of expected profundity that exempts it from the petty consistencies of accuracy; it is meant to be "poetic." It is given prime-time exposure because it is "meaningful." But what it really is, is a vile exculpation of the guilty and an obscene blaming of innocents. It is a warped picture of terror. It is an embarrassment to common sense, historical fact and journalistic integrity. And it is what the editors of our national news saw fit to broadcast less than a day after my son and seven others had been brutally murdered by an Arab, a fervent Muslim, intent on killing Jews. I give thanks that at least I do not own a television.

CHAPTER FIVE:
DEATH BY INTERVIEW

Where is God, you ask? Wherever we let Him in.

RABBI MENAHEM MENDEL MORGENSTERN,
THE KOTSKER REBBE

The Israeli mainstream media is a reasonable reflection of the country's make-up: mostly secular, but aware that it operates in a Jewish environment. Thus, one can wake up at 6:00 a.m. to the recitation of Shema Yisrael, a basic morning prayer, on state radio; view discussions of the week's Torah readings on television; and tune in to so-called "religious" programming on Saturday nights.

In terms of sheer volume, however, most Israeli media programming focuses on the normative Western media concerns of money, politics, sports, celebrities and sex. Most of the people involved in the production of whatever is seen, read and heard by the masses have scant knowledge of Judaism. In their minds, rabbis are for getting married, divorced and buried; kosher is something that one puts up with in the army. Sometimes experts, i.e., reporters with *kippahs*, are called in to cover "religious" stories, but other stories are just too big to leave to the second string. So, it was not odd that Israel's own Barbara Walters, Ilana Dayan, would be the one to interview Rabbi Weiss during prime time just two days after the brutal murder of six of his students. Unlike others in the media, though, Dayan was interested in listening to what her subject had to say.

Dayan's piece opens with a shot of the Mercaz HaRav campus. A dozen students are milling about in the courtyard; others, carrying books, seem to be making their way to their studies. From this very spot, she informs her viewers, she is about to broadcast a special program with the Principal of Yashlatz, Rabbi Yerahmiel Weiss—a discussion about "loss, pain and faith."

The show's opening credits roll and instead of the usual comfortable studio or well-appointed living room, the viewer sees Dayan and Rabbi Weiss seated across from each other on simple hardback chairs in the Mercaz HaRav library. Dayan holds a clipboard on her lap. After thanking her guest, she starts by stating that her goal for this interview is to discover what "happened deep within the soul" of the rabbi and his students.

For nearly half an hour, Dayan, the blonde epitome of the intelligent, secular Israeli faces the grey-bearded rabbi. Ironically, the two are dressed in nearly matching outfits—dark suits with open-necked shirt collars pulled over their jackets' lapels. They sit, one across from the other, the library's books their only scenery.

In response to Dayan's questioning, Rabbi Weiss describes going to identify the bodies. For him this was the most difficult task of what Dayan calls "that accursed night", and it is seared into his memory. He knew which of his students were missing. He knew that there were some unidentified hospitalized students. Still, "the heart tends toward hope," he explains to Dayan. But one after the other, opening the body bags (here his voice breaks), "I see, they are all mine."

Did you feel your strength ebbing?

No.

Really?

Dayan is incredulous.

No. This wasn't the issue at all. It was the pain of loss, of leaving them.

Dayan asks whether he remembers any last conversations with the murdered, "who were literally *your* students until just this last Thursday." Of course he does. Yehonadav, who had graduated from high school the previous summer, had been his charge for four years.

And there was...we called him ADaM, Avraham David Moses. He sat with me on Wednesday night in my room for a long discussion to help him with all sorts of things, with his family, a broken family...and we talked for an entire evening."

And have you spoken since then with his parents?

Of course.

What do you say to the parents of a child, a small boy like this?

The rabbi just shrugs and says, "Not much. You hug them, take them under your wing and you tell them that just yesterday you spoke with him." Rabbi Weiss speaks, too, of the need for his students to cry.

Crying is one of the healthy necessities of life. One who

doesn't feel, doesn't cry. One who doesn't cry, doesn't feel. How can you lose six students and not cry!? You would have to be made of stone!

And this is what you told your students?

He nods.

I am crying. You can cry with me.

In response to another question, Rabbi Weiss tells her that "… there is confusion, there is pain." And now it comes out: "The loss of life is the loss of faith." Suddenly it seems that Dayan has what she has been waiting for. Excited for the first time, she leans forward, exclaiming, "This is exactly what I want to explore with you!" Dayan recalls the moving eulogy that Rabbi Weiss delivered on Friday morning: "In front of thousands of students, and the dead students, wrapped in *tallitot*, lying before you… you were having a private conversation with God." Rabbi Weiss tells her that he was in a space where he saw the "complexity of life, between bewilderment and the question." His voice catching, he asks, "Why? Why have You forsaken me?"

Is this permitted, Rabbi Weiss?

It is imperative. Between this and the certainty that everything is correct, everything is true…that's where I was.

You rebuked God. You said, "What joy You have arranged for yourself in heaven for the month of Adar."

Rabbi Weiss interrupts. "No, no." He wants to explain himself. And Dayan admits that she and the rest of the media, for all their concern, for all the attention focused on the yeshivah, have been "despite it all, looking from the outside in." She can't fathom how a few moments before he had asked why God had left him he could also tell the parents, "God gives and God takes." How do both of these statements fit together?

> *This is just it. It is imperative that they do. To ask, to cry out and to weep. This is to ask God to give me back what was lost. I don't ask from a distance, but like you ask a father or mother, "Why are you leaving me now?"...I said [to God], "In Your Torah it is written, 'When Adar begins joy increases' and I need that joy that You promised me".*

Dayan asks whether any of the students may be going through a crisis of faith. "Can the students permit themselves to come to you and demand, 'Where was God on Thursday night!?'"

This is the big question. This is what her audience wants to know. Rabbi Weiss can only agree that yes, they can, and yes, the question *is* so simple. "How can one not ask? They pray, they study and in the end, they die...they are killed?"

If this is *the* question, one might expect Dayan to demand the answer, just as she would from a businessman whose shady books she has uncovered. But she remains silent. She looks at the rabbi and steers the conversation away. To revenge, to politics.

There is an odd disconnect here. The interview takes a sharp turn away from the precipice of questions to which there are no answers and instead, Dayan seeks firmer footing on more familiar ground: action against the Arabs, against the state. This is something that she can fathom. Here is the Dayan everyone knows, pushing for answers, not giving up. No more fascinated listening; instead, it's time for hard-boiled journalism. However, near the end of the interview, the conversation wends its way back to murkier waters. Rabbi Weiss describes the Sabbath he just had.

81

We try on the Sabbath to leave mourning behind. This seems superficial, but it is something deep that gives us much strength. It is impossible to forget, it is impossible to leave it [the pain of what happened] behind, but... [we regard] it from a space of agreement, a space of acceptance, a space....

Dayan interrupts.

Agreement!? Agreement with what?! With the loss of eight such young lives?! Agree with what? Futility? Meaninglessness? With this death which was completely needless? Agree with what?

With the 300 living [students]. With the fact that the Jewish people live on. I agree with life's hopes....

Excuse me, but I must interrupt, I want to understand you, not argue...Isn't there something in the [acceptance of this loss which] negates the holiness of the deceased, the importance of the individuals who died?

Rabbi Weiss tries to explain.

...I am happy that the world continues, with my grandchildren's smile...that I continue to live...But now you ask me, because I accept God's decree, don't I anull something else? I wish that I knew that I was sanctifying the One who made this decree. Maybe he [each victim] was chosen to be some sort of atonement for us all. I can't say anything about such matters. They are beyond our intellect. ... The keys of death and life are in the hands of God. We are not there.

Dayan seems to be probing for a chink in the armor. Where is the crack, even the tiniest one, in this rabbi's faith? How can it still be intact after the horror, right here in this library, of only a few evenings ago? She asks what will remain with him from that fateful Thursday. "Pain," he answers, his eyes closing to hold back the tears.

With an empathetic nod, Dayan asks, "Have you already begun to miss the children themselves?" The tears come now. Rabbi Weiss can only nod, he cannot speak. Sniffling, the words catching in his throat, he is the most visibly shaken that he has been over the entire interview. And Dayan, gently, yes, but on the mark, moves right in.

Is this a longing that faith can heal?"

This is something different altogether. Faith is the reckoning with God, not with one's loss. From the perspective of faith...

As Rabbi Weiss launches into his explanation, the screen alternates between close up shots of Rabbi Weiss and footage of yeshivah students praying. As the rabbi speaks, the bearded students slowly sway, deep in prayer.

Life begins with He who gives it and life does not end. It escapes from its corporeal burden and continues in some other place...For us, death is the most difficult of things. We spend our entire lives trying to escape from the terror of death. Actually, we don't always live our lives in the fullest, most positive, sense because we are busy trying to escape death...But we know that there is a positive place where life continues. I am convinced, even in my own limited understanding, that it's there...Life returns to that place.

Dayan cannot take leave without probing this issue once more.

I ask myself and I ask you, Rabbi Weiss, one final question: Within all this bubble of faith and values which surrounds you, and with all that you know, all that you studied and all that you taught over the years and which seem to be helping you survive these troubling days, wasn't there a moment over this weekend that you reached a breaking point?

I'll answer you from an unexpected place—a place of faith.

Rabbi Weiss pauses, gathering his thoughts, fighting back tears. He worries that on some level of divine providence maybe he was in some way responsible for the death of his students.

I thought, that if this place is hit so hard, perhaps it is not fitting that I should stand at its head. Maybe somebody better...maybe he would not be struck. Or, if I'm so good that I get hit, then I also shouldn't be here.

The camera lingers for a few seconds on the rabbi's silent, pained face. Dayan begins her conclusion but the camera stays focused on Rabbi Weiss' bearded visage.

Despite this, it seems to me that the Yeshivah LeTze'irim students have merited an outstanding rabbi and educator. I thank you for agreeing to be with us this evening.

This interview made something of a hero out of Rabbi Weiss. It had an impact on the country's secular majority who, like Dayan, had been following the horrific events surrounding the massacre "looking from the outside in." Rabbi Weiss opened a window for them. With great presence and, more importantly, with honest humility, he explained what he felt and what he thought.

On a certain level, though, Dayan was more interesting to me than

Rabbi Weiss. As her questions made clear, she had a very specific agenda. She, the investigative reporter, was searching for a failure, looking for the place where the rabbi's faith would give out. Again and again she pressed him as to whether he had "reached a breaking point", whether he had felt his "strength ebbing." She demanded to know how one could dare to accept death without pointing an accusatory finger at the Almighty. She challenged his belief, asking, "Where was God?" Yet, at the critical moment, she faltered and withdrew instead of pressing on. The learned rabbi agreed with her that the question of where God was while these innocent children were being murdered needed to be asked— "How can one *not* ask?" he admitted. I still wonder why she didn't demand an answer, instead of veering off into politics.

Why was it so important to her to search for a chink in the rabbi's faith? And why did she ultimately not force the issue when she had the chance? On one level, her questioning seems to echo an all-too-common reaction that people have when faced with an individual who appears to be claiming higher moral ground. Reactively, we often try to point out the inconsistencies of his position. The omnivore points to the vegetarian's leather shoes, the businessman peppers the idealistic student with queries about tuition payments. It is difficult to accept difference—especially that which paints our own actions and habits as less worthy than another's. Almost instinctively, we try to cut them down to size. But, I believe that something else took place that Sunday night in the library.

Dayan, sitting across from Rabbi Weiss, wearing nearly the same outfit, coincidentally looking almost like some photographic negative of the rabbi, played the foil to his religious belief. She represented, as she said, those looking from the outside in: the secular. For some Israelis, this secularism is marked not only by minimal religious practice but by a conscious (and often proud) atheism. This stems partly from Israeli society's socialist ethos, from her early leaders' struggle to replace heavenly grace with human sweat. But, I believe, the lack of faith is also rooted in something else.

Nearly every Israeli has tasted the bitter taste of tragic loss. Nearly everyone here knows somebody who has lost a son, or daughter, or parent or sibling to war and terror. The eternal question of evildoing under God's watch is far from merely theoretical here. The pain of loss is all too real. For some secular, I imagine, the pain of facing this loss is too bitter to admit the sweetening effect that faith in a good, just, and loving God might offer. Dayan couldn't understand how Rabbi Weiss could leave his pain and sorrow behind for the Sabbath rest. She was shocked and expressed the notion that perhaps this behavior constituted an affront to the memory of the deceased, that it dis-acknowledged the pain of loss.

This stems from a misunderstanding of what it means to believe, to be religious. Dayan was relating to faith as a simplistic black-and-white ideology: Either having faith in God should engender blissful acceptance of all that the world throws one's way and mute all pain, or else–if one suffers–then one cannot believe. And in the face of the horrible death of so many young innocents, a tragedy that would make anyone want to rage against the dying of the light, how could one not feel pain? And so, how could one believe?

This is why Dayan was astounded at the rabbi's equilibrium. She could not fathom how he could be, quantum-physics-like, in two states at once. While still painfully mourning the death of his students, he found consolation in his faith that somewhere else, beyond the realm of human understanding, a reason for the tragedy exists. That somewhere else life goes on. Rabbi Weiss is willing to defer judgment. He believes that, yes, the Almighty is just and good—but we cannot understand His ways. For the rabbi, consolation comes from knowing that, not withstanding our own ignorance, there *is* an answer to be had, a reason to be found.

Is this why Dayan did not continue to press Rabbi Weiss? The fact that someone believes, even if she doesn't, may be comforting in itself. It raises the hope, however slim, that perhaps all is not lost. This is something that the religious provide the secular—a glimmer of possible order in a chaotic world. Perhaps, even as Dayan was looking for chink in the armor, she was hoping not to find it. Perhaps Dayan did not want to undo this link to some larger Truth, wherever it may be.

As for myself, this give and take on faith, on causality, on the question of God's role in the face of evil, was not one which occupied my thoughts. I never found myself wondering where God was that night. Evil exists because Man exists; it thrives where Man denies the godly within himself. I never found myself troubled by my lack of understanding any master plan in the seeming chaos of "meaningless death." My own understanding of God's place vis-à-vis human suffering leans less in the direction of theodicy and more towards accepting that even in our worst pain, God does not abandon us.

Suffering, death, our seemingly endless capacity to inflict the most heinous of ills upon each other—they are our lot. Some will choose to do evil, because we humans are free to choose. God's promise to us, at least until the Messiah arrives, is not an end to this world's evils, but a pledge to *be* with us throughout them.

Where was God on that accursed Thursday night? Where was the Almighty when the blood of innocents ran over the library tiles? I believe that He was with my 16-year-old son as he breathed his last prayers. God was there, welcoming Avraham David into the World to Come as the life drained out of his bullet-ridden body. God was with those trembling in fear behind the classroom door, giving them hope that their fate would not be the same as the others. God was with the young Elhanan Cohen, giving him the courage to push past the murderer so that he could return to his family. God was with Rabbi Weiss, allowing him to cry with his shocked students at the horror of it all. God was with me as I looked for the last time at my son's face. And those who wish to emulate the Holy One in His kindness can try to be there for others in the face of our own all-too-human pain and suffering.

CHAPTER SIX:
CLOAKS OF LIGHT

In the name of the Lord, the God of Israel:
On my right Michael, on my left Gavriel, before me Uriel,
behind me Raphael. Above my head, the Presence of God.

FROM THE TRADITIONAL PRAYER SAID

BEFORE RETIRING IN THE EVENING

One of the many rabbis who visited me while I was sitting shivah asked me if I had a copy of the Zohar, the basic text of Jewish mysticism, in my library. I retrieved it for him. He opened the volume and marked a place. "Look here when you have a chance, yes, here." was all he said. Weeks later I remembered his visit and began to read the Aramaic text.

Rav Aba began his homily: It is written "The Heavens are the Heavens of God, but the Earth He gave to Man" (Psalms 115). This is a verse worth inspecting. It should have read, "The Heavens are God's, but the Earth He gave to Man." Why repeat 'heavens?' Rather, we need to see that there is a heaven and there is a heaven. A lower heaven, beneath which lies an earth. An upper heaven, beneath which lies an earth. And all

*of the contents, upper and lower, all are similar, these
just like these.*

The text goes on to explain in great detail how the Ten Divine
Spheres are aligned—upper mirrored by lower, the lower
receiving their powers from the emanations of the upper. It tells of
letters that travel up and down along rivers of light that ascend and
descend between the two heavens, the two Gardens of Eden. They
shine and flicker in the light, moving back and forth, entering and
exiting the two parallel worlds, one above and one below.

I slowly made my way through the Aramaic, wondering why this
rabbi had sent me here. Then the text began to describe something
else.

*When the soul of a righteous man rises up to the Garden
of Eden these two letters leave the light and descend
upon that soul.*

But, the Zohar explains, these letters are actually chariots—
one the glowing chariot of the angel Michael, the other that of
Raphael.

*They approach the soul and say, "Come in peace, come
in peace, come in peace."*

Next, two more glowing chariots approach. They belong to the
angels Gabriel and Denoriel.

*They take the soul and enter the secret hall of the
Garden—called Divinity. There, twelve species of spices
are hidden...and there are all the souls' garments, an
appropriate one for every individual soul to wear, each
tailor-made. And woven into these garments are the good
deeds that each soul did in this world. Every [good deed]
is part of the garment. They [the angels] proclaim, "This*

is the garment of so-and-so," and they take that garment and dress that righteous soul in the Garden with his proper clothing, just as one would in this world...

Once dressed, the soul is directed to its proper place. Then the chariots depart.

...

In this heaven are twenty-two letters, each dripping dew. With this dew the souls are bathed and are healed.... And they in turn pour this dew upon those who learn Torah in our world with no expectation of reward....and the souls in turn are nourished with this dew.

Then the text describes how the souls ascend from this heaven to the next, where they glow and bask in the divine light of the upper heaven.

How wonderful the portion of those souls who are dressed in their garments, the garments worn by the righteous in the Garden of Eden. These garments made of the good deeds done by men in this world, in accordance with the commandments of the Torah. This is how the souls exist in the lower Garden, in these fine clothes.

But, when a soul ascends to the upper heavens, it is granted garments even finer than these. These are woven out of the individual's will and his heart's intent during study and prayer. For this will rises up, crowning He who it crowns, but some remains for that individual, out of which will be made the garment of light to dress his soul when it ascends above.

Yes, even though these lower garments depend upon

actions, the upper garments depend upon nothing but the soul's desire, all so that it [the soul] may stand among the angels, the holy spirits. This is the truth of the matter. So, Rav Shimon bar Yochai, the Holy Light, learned from Elijah: the lower garments of the earthly garden are made from deeds; the upper garments from will and the heart's intention.

It is still hard to picture my son—his blond hair shining in the light, his pale face alive with his smile—without feeling heart-rending loss. But I know that his soul resides above, cloaked in the warm light of the garments which he made for himself beforehand. Too young to have "accomplished" much in our world, I know that he strove to worship God with pure intention. Now he basks in the glow of the Divine.

I imagine my son, an overly-serious young man searching for religious perfection, who spent hour after hour pouring over holy texts. I imagine his last moments. He crouches between the stacks of holy books to which he had committed his every waking moment, hearing the shots ringing out, hearing the screams of those already dying, waiting for the murderer to make his way to his row, with no escape. I imagine my sixteen-year-old, who had not yet shaved, who had never kissed a girl, who awoke before dawn each morning to pray, I imagine him preparing for his own death. His heart's intentions—pure love for the Holy One, pure longing for the world-to-come. And as the bullets tear through his thin frame, as the blood leaves his body, above they are weaving his garments of light. As the sirens wail and we search in shock, the angels are busy gathering up the last threads of my son's holy intent. Those still immersed in Torah study, who have not yet heard the news and shut their books in horror, are anointed with heavenly dew. And as they dance in Gaza with murderous delight, throwing candies to children at the news of eight more dead Jews, above the glowing garments are waiting; waiting for my son, Avraham David Moses.

CHAPTER SEVEN:
LETTERS

All Israel is responsible for one another.

TALMUD SANHEDRIN 27b

After the week of shivah was over, I went to pick up my mail. The mailbox was full to overflowing with condolence letters. Over the next few weeks and months more would arrive—hundreds of letters in all. Some were from old family friends. There were several from Israelis who sent poems and pamphlets in addition to their condolences. There would eventually be a number of books that had been dedicated to the memory of the eight murdered students. The vast majority of mail, though, was from American yeshivah students: some from youngsters in grade school, some from older high school students—mostly teenage girls.

These letters often described, in more or less detail, how the students had heard of the attack and how it affected them. Many writers stressed their own identification with the victims—they too were teenage yeshivah students. They expressed their shock, their horror and their wishes for consolation. Some sought to empathize by telling me stories of their own experiences with death—a lost parent or grandparent. Some admitted that they had nothing to say, yet wanted to let me know that they wished me well. Many wrote about their own theological understandings of good and evil. They told me how God's plans were unfathomable, how my son was surely seated next to God's throne now. One boy even quoted Bob Marley—"Everything's goin' to be alright." Some young writers sent their telephone numbers and addresses, hoping, I guess, that correspondance with an American teenager would offer me a measure of condolence unavailable elsewhere. This still makes me smile.

But what was most touching about these letters was the measure of *fraternity* they expressed. Time after time, in letter after letter, these youngsters wrote how, despite the distance, as Jews, they felt that my loss was their loss as well. Some boys even signed as "your brother." Many told me of their plans to dedicate something (be it charity, some Torah study, recitation of psalms) to the memory of my son and the other victims. I believed them when they wrote of how shaken the news of the attack had left them and of how they needed to find some way of turning that horror into something more positive. For some reason, one of the the letters that touched me most was from a teenage girl who wrote that after hearing the terrible news she went to pray for the first time in two years. An act straight from the Psalmist's words, "Out of the depths, I called to You...."

There is something special about our tribe. We are a people bound together by ties that span time and place. We are a family. But this reaction—this outpouring of empathy, of wanting to acknowledge our pain and do something with it—also gives me pause to reflect about these family ties. Perhaps it should be no surprise that the majority of the letters I received were from Orthodox Jewish youth, studying in Orthodox Jewish schools. Geography aside, they shared the most with the attack's teenage victims. It was sadly all too easy for them to identify with my son and the others.

However, I also wonder whether this small, select group perhaps feels more strongly attached to the Jewish nation than those whose religious commitment is more moderate. Now, I know of many exceptionally committed Jews who are not religiously inclined in the least. But overall, daily study, daily prayer, keeping kosher, keeping the Sabbath—how can these not affect one's connection to *Am Yisrael*? Lacking the immersion that halakhic religion mandates, well…thoughts and feelings often follow action and not the reverse. Those who may argue for Jewish culture, for Jewish ethnicity, for Jewish peoplehood removed from religion are welcome to do so. I wish them well in attaining what it is that they want.

Responding to Naftali Moses' personal loss is surely no litmus test of anything. However, for better or worse, I am not sure that even strongly ethnically-identified Italian-Americans would react with as much vicarious pain to news of, say, earthquake victims in the "old country" as these youths did to the murder of eight boys at Mercaz HaRav. While Donne's moving meditation on humankind reflects a noble sense of universal belonging, in reality bells toll in different pitches and those attuned to a particular pitch hear that bell more clearly than others. That tuning in, which is neither automatic nor easily achieved, demands daily effort.

CHAPTER EIGHT:
GUARDING MEMORY

*Three things were preordained, and if they weren't, they should
have been: that the dead rot, that the dead will be forgotten
from our hearts, and that produce decomposes.*

TALMUD PESAHIM 54b

The elementary school where Avraham David and his friend
Segev studied (and where my son Elisha Dan was in sixth
grade at the time of the attack) has had its share of trying times.
A number of its young students' parents had died, whether from
illness or terror, leaving no small amount of work for those
children's teachers and classmates who tried, as best they could,
to help. My son and Segev, however, each the kind of student that
is a teacher's pleasure to teach, each with a brother still studying
there, had been the first graduates to perish.

Given the mandatory military draft upon graduation from high
school, it is not uncommon for Israeli schools, especially high
schools, to have memorial boards or corners dedicated to deceased
graduates. Those that have not lost graduates to the many wars
are probably the exception. About six months after the attack, my
son's former elementary school unveiled a beautiful glass plaque

engraved with the boys' images and some words about their death. It was hung in a central location that allows children to stop and read about these two martyred tenth-graders who once studied where they do now.

The night after I was first shown the plaque, I dreamed about it. In my dream, I am in a wooded grove together with other members of an anonymous group. We are all standing around my son's coffin in a clearing. The plaque from school hangs on a tree. A gentle rain begins to fall. I am concerned that this outdoor memorial is not safe—that the rain will wash something away. I wonder why we are outside, exposed to the elements.

For me the meaning of this dream is not hard to fathom. I am concerned about preserving my son's memory. I worry that the public aspect of memorialization is wearing away at something better kept safe inside. I am torn between the commonness of public memorial and the privacy of personal memory. I fret about how to balance them, how to keep the private viable, nourished with oxygen, without eroding it from exposure. Throughout the year spent mourning my son's murder, this tension, manifested in a variety of ways, has been difficult for me. As one of a group— the eight Mercaz HaRav victims—my son, in the very moment of his death, lost a privacy that is disturbing to me. Afterwards, in my mourning, I feel pressed upon, even confronted by this loss— alongside the exponentially larger loss of my son himself. Memory is all that is left of my beloved first-born boy. The idea that I might lose his memory, too, is too terrible to contemplate.

I know that being a divorced father made me more sensitive to this issue. I needed to fight long and hard to ensure that I would remain in my sons' lives, and they in mine, when my marriage to their mother ended. The final settlement was that my two sons from my first marriage would live with me half-time. Joint custody is rare in Israel—most divorced mothers are granted the equivalent of sole custody over their children. Divorced fathers pay large amounts of child support, but the amount of time they can spend with their own children depends almost entirely upon their ex-wife's good will. I had invested a huge amount of effort to ensure that I wouldn't be one of those fathers whose children grew up barely knowing him— thinking of him more (as one social worker put it to me) as "an uncle" than a parent. I remain convinced that children need two involved parents, and children of divorce all the more so. In my view, joint custody is the best possible arrangement for divorced children and their parents. I treasured the time I had together with my two boys and rearranged my life in order to be home with them for the half-week they lived with me. After my son's death, though, through numerous comments, I learned that Avraham David's mother had anguished over what she had experienced as the terrible loss of her children to shared custody with their father.

I already knew that many others were genuinely appalled that despite the divorce, I had had the gall to actually want to remain as close as possible to my own sons. I frequently dealt with snide remarks and raised eyebrows. Time after time, whether trying to rearrange army reserve duty or talk to a doctor about one of my boys' care, I was given the clear message that as a divorced father, I must clearly be the secondary parent. (Happily, my children's school system was almost always a wonderfully inclusive exception to this).

After my son's death, because my son had two sets of parents, things were also, at times, more complicated. Sometimes this meant that two family representatives, one from each side, were called upon to say a few words or light a candle, instead of one. Not a big deal. What was more disturbing, though, related not only to being a divorced parent, but with sharing the tragedy of my loss with the public, was the feeling I had experienced in my dream. I worried about protecting my son's memory; about keeping it from being washed away by the commonness of public martyrdom. He was not just a symbol, but a person—a unique individual whom I loved dearly. These protective feelings resonated with the same anxiety that I had felt when, during our divorce, I was fighting the efforts of my ex-wife to retain sole custody of our children. I worried that another fight was brewing—if not for custody over my son, then over his memory.

While still sitting *shivah*, I was approached by someone from our local community newsletter to write a memorial piece for the next issue—due out in less than a week. I was taken aback by this poorly timed intrusion. I said as much and suggested that we talk after the *shivah*. I was surprised by the editor's insistence, but I repeated that I would be in touch with him after the *shivah*.

That evening, a friend of mine came over and explained to me that my son's stepfather had written a long "Letter to Avraham David" which was scheduled to be published in the coming newsletter. My friend had already spoken with the editor about pushing this off—but the editor had been insistent in his refusal. I felt, as did my friend, that this was a type of blackmail. Of course, I *could* remain silent and let *someone else* write about my son as his own…. Or I could add something myself. I felt as if without my own input, someone else's memory of my beloved son was going to become the "official record" of who he was and what he meant. This was upsetting. Although I wasn't pleased about it, that night I took out my laptop, sat in my low-to-the-ground mourner's chair, and with the help of two friends with better Hebrew writing skills than mine, composed a piece about my son, his loss and the retention of faith in the face of it all.

After the *shivah* was over, something even more upsetting took place. An Israeli weekly newspaper, aimed at the religious (and/ or more right-wing) public, devoted a double-page spread to moving obituaries for each of the previous week's terror victims. Something of each youth's personality and his uniqueness was described—highlighting the sadness of each loss. Instead of anything like this about Avraham David, though, there appeared a piece written by a woman commiserating with my son's mother on the *second* loss of her son. The first loss, of course, was in her divorce. The silver lining, she wrote, was that this grieving mother had fortunately remarried into a large extended family so that now her son was mourned by all her new relatives as well. There was not a word about my son himself; and, he was presented as mourned by his mother's family alone.

I was upset that this is what the paper had chose to print; that the legacy left by my son's terrible death was not the loss of his sweet smile, his brilliant mind, his religious devotion. Rather, his story was subsumed by that of his mother's trauma in divorce and her redemption through remarriage. I surmised that the obituary-cum -paean to remarriage must have been penned by a mother, surely divorced herself. Although I didn't notice the byline at first, a neighbor who had come over to gingerly check if I had seen the paper pointed out that the author was my ex-wife's sister-in-law. This writer, who was usually the paper's political reporter, was a divorcee who had remarried – to David Moriah's brother. It made better sense now. She wasn't interested in my son. In the face of this tragedy, she had found an opportunity to write about her own family and that was what she had done.

I felt cheated. I felt that I had been purposely cut out of my son's life. I was disgusted that the reporter hadn't even taken the time to talk to me. Since I live ten meters away from my ex-wife, it wouldn't have been too logistically complicated. I felt that I needed to once again fight for my connection with my son. I had a conversation with the paper's publisher (who happens to be a neighbor of mine). He told me that although he never interfered with content, he well understood my agitation and wanted to do something to make amends. I had a less pleasant conversation with the editor, who offered to print a response that I could write myself. But I was too upset to do so. My neighbor the publisher suggested that the paper write another piece at the end of the next mourning period—when a month would have passed and another ritually prescribed stage of mourning would be complete.

When the month had passed, however, I looked back at this episode with equanimity, having realized that the paper really owed me and my son nothing (and that the article that had so disturbed me was already lining the birdcages of its readers). I asked the reporter who called me up if she knew why she had been asked to do this follow-up story. She told me that she did. I described how I had felt about the original piece, how hurt I had been by it. But, I told her, there was no reason to dredge up this unpleasantness again; it would only focus attention on tensions between my ex-wife and myself, something that had nothing to do with my son's memory. "Better not to write anything," I told her. Eventually we agreed that she would talk to my ex-wife as well and write a piece that had to do only with the loss of our son, and not us. She did, and the piece appeared on the day we unveiled his tombstone, the words on which were chosen together by both his parents.

Here rests the martyr
Avraham David Moses *(may God avenge his blood)*
Son of Naftali and Rivka
Heaven Fearing, Sensitive, Loving and Beloved
Devoted to Torah Study
Murdered while Applying Himself to his Study
A Torah Scroll Clasped to his Breast

This episode convinced me that I should not expect anybody else to memorialize my son in ways that I felt were appropriate. The only one who could do that was me. Throughout the year after Avraham David's death, I would often feel battered by the memorial ideas, initiatives and programs that others would sometimes offer, sometimes foist upon me. As a parent grieving over the still too-fresh loss of a beloved child, this was one of the more difficult trials the year presented.

CHAPTER NINE:
HISTORY VERSUS MY STORY

*To be a truthful chronicler is to be a perfect historical
seismograph, to record accurately the vibrations of history.
But a seismograph does not tell us what it is like to be in an
earthquake. For that we need a moral witness.*

AVISHAI MARGALIT, *THE ETHICS OF MEMORY*

History and memory can be intimate friends or bitter enemies.
The first, history, is something compiled. It is researched, it
is conspicuously created—yet it often lays claim to the ontological
weight of unassailable fact, giving the impression that it is the
definitive account of what took place. Memory is more personal,
experiential. To ask someone, "What do you remember of that
night?" is a different question than "What happened?" The former
calls for introspection; the latter, investigation. Memory may or
may not be shared, but history has a commonality that memory
does not always possess. And that is the problem. History, carefully
crafted and publicized, may in fact exclude the personal memories
of those intimately connected to the very events that it purports to
describe.

History, no matter how recorded, has potential for moving the past into the present and future. There it can be learned, taught, discussed and debated. Memory, though, like love, needs nurturing lest it fade into the nothingness of endless, expansive time. Memorialization, whether in stone or song, aims at fixing memory. Like the silver bromide once used in photographic development, it is the additive which attempts to hold on to the past, lest it vanish, leaving only a shadow so faint and thin, that you ask yourself, "Was it ever really here?" If mourning is the internal, personal marking of loss, memorial is an almost oxymoronic attempt at constructing some outer edifice to make present that which no longer exists. It is a manifestation of lack.

Memorials – be they ceremonies, books, statues, paintings or other – attempt to move memory into history's realm by constructing a mass, a weight, a presence, for the cobweb thin strands of memory. By concretizing memory, the memorial moves it out of the inner folds of the psyche into a more accessible—and usually public—space. Yet the move from the abstract memory of what was, to a physical representation may be awkward, even disturbing. You look for a picture to frame. Do you choose the candid shot or the posed? While each of them are of the same subject, while any may objectively reflect the loved one you lost, not all of them reflect your memory. Not all, if any, convey what *you* remember, what you *want* to keep remembering, what you want memorialized. The public space, the space where history reigns, can never do justice to his memory or to your treasured memories.

A person, even a child, is his own being—full of feelings, notions, desires, ambitions—that are his alone. Yet once gone, what remains? Perhaps, if he built a business, ran a hospital, designed a plane—those things upon which he left his mark stand as a memorial to the person who was. But what if he was only a boy, who had still not ventured beyond the walls of school? His memory resides in those who knew him. And the longing and pain of loss, at times nearly too heavy a burden to bear for those who miss him, rests on those gossamer threads of remembrances. And lest they tear, loosening the burden they can barely support, sending all that is left tumbling into endless oblivion, the unending wasteland of the forgotten, those memories are shared with others in hopes of strengthening them, in order to spread the burden over a greater area.

Yet what becomes of memory shared? Does it move into the realm of history, that public space which is open to interpretation, argumentation, differences of opinion? To whom does it then *belong*? Who decides what will be recalled? What forgotten? What etched into the public record and made into history? And what left out, to fall by the wayside of time: to grow dusty, neglected, abandoned, gone forever? What claims can be made on the vapor wisps of memory—all that is left of your beloved—by those who knew him less, if at all?

A month after we had buried him, a small crowd gathered again at my son's grave, this time for the "unveiling." A long granite slab had been laid over his too-young, too-delicate body buried in the cool brown earth of Gush Etzion. We gathered around his grave to recite psalms. I sobbed into the chest of a friend and then, each of us leaving a small stone behind, we all returned home to prepare for the Sabbath.

Two days later, we were invited to take part in the first of many public events intent on memorializing my son and the other boys who had been murdered. This was a *hakhnassat sefer Torah*—the installation of a Torah scroll at the Mercaz HaRav Yeshivah. This particular scroll had been purchased by an Israeli businessman who lived down the block from the yeshivah. Even though over the years he had had little to do with the yeshivah, after the previous month's events he had felt the need to do *something*. The dedication of a Torah scroll (which takes a year to write by hand with a quill pen and costs upwards of $20,000) is a traditional Jewish means of memorialization. Usually, the last few lines of Hebrew script are not fully written out before the ceremony. They are only outlined so that the words can be filled in and the writing of the scroll completed as part of the ceremony. Then the scroll is dressed in its mantle and paraded with music and dancing under a *huppah*—a canopy, the same as that used for a wedding—to its destination, usually a synagogue, where it will be read from for the first time.

My family and I made the rookie mistake of arriving on time. In the parking lot of an apartment building near the yeshivah, a large tent had been set up. Inside, a scribe was seated at a table on which the Torah scroll lay. Dozens of people milled about—youngsters, rabbis, men and women of all descriptions—in a semi-carnival atmosphere which reminded me of the night I had arrived at the yeshivah only thirty days before. And we waited. We waited for the other boys' families to arrive. We waited for so-and-so to complete a letter of the scroll. We waited in line to use the bathroom. We tried to keep my daughters entertained. We milled about with the rest of the crowd.

And then a van, covered with colored, flashing lights and brimming with loudspeakers—looking something like a larger, gaudier, electrified version of a 1960s psychedelic "hippie wagon"—arrived. Accompanied by the lively, ear-splitting music that poured forth from an array of mobile speakers, we were off. This raucous, garish procession wound its way through the streets of Kiryat Moshe around the yeshivah. My young daughters enjoyed being part of this fantastically tawdry parade. From her vantage point on my shoulders, my nearly-four-year-old was mesmerized by the lights and my seven-year-old marched along—sometimes with me, sometimes with her mother on the sidelines. Yeshivah youth danced alongside us as we wended our way around the long block to the yeshivah.

At some point, I ducked out of the procession and made my way to the yeshivah where eventually everyone arrived, the Torah was read and we ended up in the yeshivah's dining room for a catered dinner. None of Avraham David's high school friends were there—there was not enough room for them at the party. I sat next to a friend's son-in-law who was studying at Mercaz. He pointed out who was who in the yeshivah pantheon seated on the dais. A little while later, Benyamin Netanyahu, then parliamentary opposition head, arrived and I watched as he hobnobbed with the rabbis, the donor and assorted bigwigs seated beside him.

Watching Netanyahu smilingly refuse our host's offer of a plate laden with stringy chicken and over-cooked vegetables, I asked myself what I was doing here. I hoped that this display of "taking back the night" had somehow helped the yeshivah students gain some closure. As for myself, I sat surrounded by strangers. I looked around and realized that we were sitting in the same room to which I had been led a month before to identify my son's body. It hadn't been obvious to me at first—what with all the people, tables and food. Then it had been empty save for the plastic-encased body lying on a table. I couldn't remember if the other bodies had also been there or only my son's. I do remember that when they pulled back the plastic from his face I had wanted to give him one last kiss on the head. But I didn't. Instead I just studied his pale face for the very last time.

Was our celebration here now some kind of vindication? A victory of the spirit over terror? Or was it just a macabre piece of busywork aimed at doing *something, anything*, to wash away last month's terrible stains and enable life to go on? I didn't have a clear answer, so I gathered up my exhausted children and wife from the women's section and we left, driving home in silence. A few weeks later, my wife, a poet, would write this:

THE WEDDING CANOPY

One day
I thought
there'd be a chuppah
and a bride.

We'd sing
and dance
and take you
toward
your future.

One day
after 30 days
of mourning there was a
chuppah
but no bride.

We sang
and danced
and took a Torah Scroll
to your school.

I thought
there'd be a chuppah
and we'd
celebrate
your life.

I was wrong.
There was a chuppah
and we
celebrated
your death.

As time went on, people began to phone and write us with invitations to more and more events in memory of "the eight martyrs." There was a synagogue that was holding a memorial cantorial Shabbat (compete with choir) and wanted "the families" to be guests of honor. It seemed that the more I politely tried to say thank you, but…, the more the organizers felt that they needed to explain how much they were sure this would be something I couldn't possibly miss. (Cantorial music holds the same place in my heart as a visit to the dentist, so I remained unconvinced). We were invited to another Torah installation (only a three hour's drive from home), a gathering in a small development town organized by the local religious council, the dedication of a hasidic study center, the establishment of a charitable fund in my son's name, a book launch which would now be dedicated to…

All sorts of people wanted to do *something* in the boys' memory and it was difficult to politely explain why I felt like staying away. Our two local elementary schools dedicated their annual joint Bible quiz (in which my son had won third place two years earlier) in memory of him and Segev Avihayil. They hinted that we might want to donate something to cover the costs, let's say, of the prizes. This was something that my wife actually decided to do, feeling that it expressed the close connection Avraham David had to Bible study. (His last teacher had related how he would catch misquoted biblical verses in the rabbinic texts that they were studying). I bowed out of actually attending the hours-long quiz by playing the too-grieving parent card.

The neighboring regional council, which included the town in which Segev Avihayil had lived, was proud to be sponsoring a large Mishnah quiz for the entire Jerusalem-area school district.

This was a plum: a rare opportunity to showcase Gush Etzion to many who wouldn't ordinarily come to a "settlement." They too decided to dedicate it to the local boys' memories. Someone spoke with me on the phone about attending, but closer to the event I forgot the date and scheduled a job interview for that morning in Tel Aviv. The organizers were livid. "What do mean you're not coming?!" I explained that I hadn't received the promised written invitation, had forgotten the exact date, and now had other commitments. "Impossible! Everyone else received theirs!" (Mine would arrive a few days later.) I tried to explain that the ways of our mail service are mysterious, but the woman I spoke to would have none of that. She couldn't believe that I was not going to attend. After all that they had done! (Of course, the event was probably planned a year before the Mercaz massacre, but they had gone to the trouble of adding a line to the program....) There went a good piece of their window dressing—the grieving father, barely back on his feet, so solicitously invited by us....

All the brouhaha didn't feel like it really had much to do with my son. He had spent the last months of his too-short life immersed in nearly round-the-clock Torah study, sleeping and eating only enough so that he'd have the strength to return to his learning. I had argued with him a few months before his death about joining us on a family Hanukah vacation. He only agreed to come once I promised that we would study together on the drive down to the desert field school and back, and that during the time we were there I would drop him off at a yeshivah every morning so that he could study while the rest of us hiked. At best, he would have been bemused by all the wasted time devoted to his memory. I wondered if, had his friends been killed and he survived, he would have danced alongside the psychedelic van or just rededicated and redoubled his already voracious Torah study in memory of those who had died.

As the year went on, "the families" were invited to meet with Knesset members debating the fate of "our" terrorist's still-standing house, talk with visiting overseas rabbis, look over a model for a large outdoor statue and attend yet more Torah installations in various venues. I passed on most of these. Something about the horrendous death of these boys made people reach out and try to mark the loss. By dedicating books or events, by designing statues, people wanted to memorialize the students. But nearly none of the memorializers knew the victims. They had no memories of these boys— they had only their own shock and some second-hand knowledge from the press.

What drove so many people to propose so many memorial events? A common reaction was voiced by one of the ZAKA volunteers who had been at Mercaz HaRav on the night of the attack. (ZAKA is a haredi organization dedicated to the identification of bodies and collection of their parts at terror and natural disaster sites.) The volunteer told a reporter that the Mercaz site was particularly difficult, even for some of the organization's most grizzled veterans. It wasn't the blood or the bodies that so disturbed these volunteers. It was the fact that the boys could have easily been their own children, shot down while studying in yeshivah. There was a too-close-for-comfort identification with the young victims and with us, their families, that drove many to look for ways to respond.

For me, though, the gaping hole torn in my heart by my son's death was too raw to find solace in any of the memorial events planned by others. I felt intruded upon by these truly well-meaning strangers with their ceremonies and Torah scrolls and after-the-fact dedications. I was still transfixed by loss, and here they were, ready to start rebuilding—on top of, what for me, were the still-warm ashes of my child. It felt like an affront to *my* memories of *my* son.

If memorialization is usually intended to strengthen fragile memories of the dead, it seemed to me that in these instances, where memory was second-hand to begin with, the various memorial projects were artificially *manufacturing* something else out of these boys, out of my own flesh and blood. With no intimate knowledge of Avraham David to work with, it was all too easy for the memorializers to fall back on a one-dimensional depiction of my son as "the martyr," "a hero," even "a tzaddik." The fullness of who he was—a complicated and gifted teenager, a joy and an exasperation, a shining light in my life about whom I worried to no end—all this seemed to be fading into the background of more convenient labels. I felt that his memory was being flattened into a poster-thin image of who he once was. This was not how I wanted to remember my son.

A teacher of Avraham David's who visited us during the *shivah* was incredulous when I told him that the angel-faced, gifted student who had soaked up his lessons like a sponge, had just a few months before been dueling with his younger brother in our living room, smashing *sukkah* poles together over the furniture. "No, not Avraham David. It couldn't be." Of course it could: He was a *person*, not a parable. My *son*, damn it—not a poster-child for some notion of a religious ideal in death as in life.

CHAPTER TEN:
EXALTATION

Prayer requests that the soul fulfill its role.

RABBI AVRAHAM YITZHAK HAKOHEN KOOK, *OLAT HARAYAH*

A mourner who attends services three times a day, will have, by the end of eleven months of saying kaddish, magnified and sanctified God's name well over 10,000 times. Kaddish, the (mostly) Aramaic prayer, has become, in the more than thousand years since its liturgical birth, the essential mourner's prayer. Scholarly tomes have been written about its history, its variations and permutations as they appear throughout Jewish liturgy. Beat poet Allen Ginsberg devoted a book to it. Theological battles (and worse) have been fought over who may say it and for whom. As a last affirmation of Jewish faith, a last statement of connection to Jewish life even at its end, a last scrap of Judaism for even those far removed from religion, there is no other prayer said as frequently and by as many different kinds of Jews as kaddish. (Even the apostate Aaron Jean-Marie Lustiger, who though born a Jew, joined the Catholic Church in his youth and climbed the ecclesiastical ladder to the rank of Cardinal by his death, insisted that kaddish be recited at his Notre Dame funeral!)

Like the unmistakable sound of plaintive tom-toms which always open those movies about Indian tribal life, the *yitgadal veyitkadash* chant of *kaddish* is immediately recognizable. Like a scent which carries with it a flood of memories long pushed to the far corners of the mind, the Aramaic cadences of *kaddish* spin an intergenerational web of connections for Jews world over.

The first *kaddish* I said for my son was recited in Jerusalem's heat with the rest of the fathers after the eulogies had come to an end. The next *kaddish* would be recited back in Efrat as I stood beside his *tallit*-wrapped body outside our local synagogue. The next, as we began to slowly walk after the ambulance which was driving him to the local cemetery. Another at the graveside. Then again at home, with the afternoon prayers. Then in synagogue on Friday night.

There were some *kaddishes* that I thought I would not complete. As the measured words I had long known by heart tumbled forth, my voice would catch and I could feel my heart constrict and the tears flow down my cheeks. Then, part sob, part prayer, the words continued, as I tried to breathe through the sobbing that wracked me with a weight of emotion I had no idea existed within me. And through the tears, the words still came—as if the rhythmic Aramaic was making its own way out of my chest, through my lips and into the world.

Months, and thousands of *kaddishes* later, I attended an interesting conference on grieving sponsored by the avowedly secular kibbutz movement. One discussion was devoted to the role of *kaddish* in secular Israeli culture. The lecturer gave a bit of the prayer's history and offered a few examples of ways in which non-believing Israeli poets and writers have struggled with its call to magnify the name of a God in whom they have little or no faith. The fact that this Aramaic prayer (not even Hebrew!), which can sound like incomprehensible religious mumbo-jumbo to the untrained ear, was afforded such pride of place in Israeli ritual was frustrating to the secularists in the room. A middle-aged woman, raised on a kibbutz, summed up the general feeling, "This is what you want to say standing on the freshly dug grave of your loved one: God is great!?" Rolling her eyes, she added in colloquial Arabic, "What a prayer!"

What a prayer. The Mourner's Kaddish consists of six short sections. It is a "call and response" between the speaker and the congregation, and in fact, may only be said in the presence of a minimal symbolic community—a quorum of ten, or *minyan*. The mourner stands and begins:

1 - Magnified and sanctified will be His great name,

   *CONGREGATION: Faithfully true.**

2 – in the world which He created according to His will. May He reign in your lives, and in your days, and in the lives of all of the house of Israel, speedily and soon, say "Faithfully true."

   CONGREGATION: Faithfully true. May His great name be forever blessed for eternity.

   MOURNER: His great name will be forever blessed for eternity.

---

* *Amen—is connected to the Hebrew root for both truth and faith. It is a word which affirms, a large "Yes!" I will leave it literally translated.*

3 – Blessed and praised and adorned and elevated and heightened and glorified and uplifted and hailed will be the name of the Holy One, blessed is He

Congregation: *Blessed is He.*

4 – above all blessings and song, praises and consolations that we utter in this world, and say, "Faithfully true."

Congregation: *Faithfully true.*

5 – There will be much peace from the heavens, and life for us and all Israel, and say, "Faithfully true."

Congregation: *Faithfully true.*

6 – The Maker of peace in His heights, He will make peace for us and all Israel, and say, "Faithfully true."

Congregation: *Faithfully true.*

What a prayer. A prayer for the mourner, still in shock, staring open-mouthed at the gaping hole torn in his life, still transfixed by the blinding headlights of death in which he has been caught.

I want to skip over the history of the evolution of *kaddish*, the obvious lack of mention of death or dying, and focus on the prayer's existential meaning, designed to be verbalized at times of crushing crisis. The mourner speaks and the assembled answer. The mourner, for whom no words can offer much solace right now, speaks and he is listened to. He is answered by his community. The assembled affirm and even repeat what he says. His words are echoed back to him, they are attested to. The repetition resonates, as corresponding words of the same frequency enhance one another. The mourner speaks ancient words, passed down through the ages, and his community listens. Then they respond in kind.

It is noteworthy that the mourner's prayer is not addressed to God, but to the community. God is only mentioned in the third person. The mourner starts by speaking to the assembled, "May He reign in *your* lives, and in *your* days…," blessing them that they should merit God's presence. By the prayer's end, though, he is speaking not *to* them, but *for* them. He prays on behalf of the community that there will be peace and life "for us". By the end of his recitation of the *kaddish*, the mourner, hanging on to this ancient Aramaic lifeline, has become more enmeshed with his community.

The *kaddish*, which gives the mourner a presence within his community, is, however, essentially a prayer of absence. It speaks of a God twice removed. While in most Jewish prayers God is addressed directly, "Blessed are You…," here, not only is God spoken of in the third person, but for the most part, it is God's *name* and not God himself which is the subject of the mourner's words, as in "May His great name be forever blessed…".

"Sanctification of God's name" or *kiddush haShem* is the normative expression used in Judaism to describe praiseworthy actions done by Jews which reflect well upon their God, and it is almost always used to describe martyrdom—giving one's life for God. The phraseology of the *kaddish*, which is concerned with "sanctifying the name of God", echoes that of *kiddush haShem* carrying with it associations of noble death, but also of other virtuous acts. However, there is still an implied distance—it is God's *name* being sanctified and not God Himself. This difference is worth examining.

In traditional Jewish discourse, the literal name of God features prominently. God is often referred to euphemistically as "the Name," since pronouncing the actual name of God is prohibited. The different names of God are held to be indicative of His various attributes, and a good portion of Jewish mysticism is ·devoted to studying the various names and their permutations. Some of the names of God are so ineffable that they were secretively passed down only to select individuals in each generation.

A name refers to something without actually *being* that thing. A name exists in the realm of language, in a community's cultural connection to the real world. But words are by definition only ephemeral ghosts of the reality to which they refer. The word "water," no matter how brilliantly evoked in the most creative language, cannot compete with the direct apprehension you get of water when a bucketful is emptied onto your head. God the Creator is the most Real there can be, yet at the same time He is also the most intangible to his creations. Naming God or referring to God's names is linguistically the closest one can get to God, while simultaneously serving as a reminder that this name-calling is not actually the Real thing. The name, so indicative as to be ineffable, is still just that—a name, and not God Himself. It is a marker of the presence of absence.

The call to sanctify God's name by the mourner is an acknowledgment of this difficult state of absent presence. This is also the temporal framework of the *kaddish*. Its language points to the future. Together with his community, the mourner offers a prayer that recognizes the lack found in the present. God's name *will be* magnified and sanctified—hopefully "speedily and soon". Eventually, there "*will be* much peace from the heavens"

and it will be God who *"will make* peace for us and all Israel."
Yet for the time being, the mourner and his community stand
on the precipice of the abyss which death has torn open in their
midst. *Right now,* the mourner can only hope that the future will
be better. *Right now,* the darkness of death has descended upon
the assembled. *Right now,* the weight of pain leaves little doubt
that we have not yet arrived at those long-awaited and wished-for
days of peace. There is no peace in the mourner's heart—only the
pieces of something that death has torn to bits.

And so, what can be said at such a time? The central section of the
kaddish admits that the answer is, essentially, nothing. The mourner
offers a long list of hoped-for future exaltations—"blessed and
praised and adorned, etc"—yet, in his next breath states that these
words, applied to God, only reflect the inadequacy of language.
For God will be praised above and beyond anything "that we utter
in this world." And that is as true a thing as can be said—that the
words of this world are empty. They crash with fury against the
rocks of our being, spewing foam into the air—yet fall back with
the tide, leaving only the smallest of traces in the sand. What do
they matter? Standing before the congregation, calling out to them,
the mourner reminds them that no, there is nothing to be said.
Maybe one day, we hope soon in the future….

But right now, as the mourner chants the *kaddish*, his speech is
a mocking testament to the distance between the present reality
and the hoped-for future. Yes, one day the mourner may find
the words to say something about the horror of his loss. But for
now, he can repeat the ancient Aramaic phrases, well-worn as old
leather boots, that his fathers said before him. For now, the rolling
cadences of *kaddish*, telling of an ancient hope that has still not
arrived, are all that he can offer. The mourner has no present. He

exists in a vacuum whose air has been sucked out by the pain of a death. But, he can reach back in time and utter the same words uttered so many times by so many before him. Words already made timeless by their age, words aimed only at a time to come. Words which readily admit of their own inadequacy, chanted back by the assembled as if uttered in the emptiness of an echo-filled canyon, they are all too reflective of his own hollowness.

What a prayer.

Chapter Eleven:
Soldiers and Citizens

Memorial day. Bitter salt is dressed up
as a little girl with flowers.
The streets are cordoned off with ropes
for the marching together of the living and the dead.

Yehuda Amichai, "Seven Laments for the War Dead," *Amen*

The public commemoration of soldiers killed in battle offers a way for society to honor the memories of those who fell. Acknowledgment and gratitude take form in granite and wood, flowers and poetry. Across the world, thanks are offered on special memorial days to those who fought for us—whether we are Russian, English, or Israeli. The fallen are not just dead men (or women), but heroes whose valor is worthy of recall. They made the "ultimate sacrifice" so that their countrymen could still enjoy this day's earthly pleasures.

Oh, that things could be so simple!

War after war has cost Israel dearly: Year after year, her young men have defended its small sliver of Middle Eastern real estate against the sea of angry Arabs intent on washing the Holy Land clean of Zionist infiltrators. While her foes have still not succeeded, the ensuing battles have taken their toll. More than 20,000 Israelis have died in the conflict over the years. But not all of the fallen were soldiers. In fact, nearly 2,500 were ordinary citizens—men, women, and children—who died not in battle, but on buses, in shops, or at school. These terror victims, like my son, may have been shot in cold blood; they may have been blown up by suicide bombers; they may have been hit by missiles shot from Gaza or Lebanon at civilian population centers.

The State of Israel moved quickly after its founding to establish an official memorial day for her fallen soldiers. It was symbolically placed immediately before Independence Day to emphasize the heavy price paid by soldiers for the state's establishment and continued survival. However, public commemoration of the "other" dead has posed a long-standing problem for the Israeli powers-that-be. Are they "war casualties," like soldiers—and so deserving of the nation's gratitude—or civilian "terror victims" and perhaps deserving only of its pity?

In 1939, armed Arab mobs stirred up by the rabid Jew-hating Mufti, Hajj Amin al-Husseinei, attacked Jewish settlements throughout the British Protectorate of Palestine. Among the many victims were a mother and her three children. They were all killed in the same attack on the village of Givaton, but were accorded dissimilar official commemoration. The mother and the oldest son, members of the pre-state defense force known as the Haganah, were recognized as "war casualties" and listed as such in state memorial records and monuments. No official mention was made of the two younger children.*

As late as 2003, when a Haifa bus was blown up, killing two

_____

* *This episode, as well as much of the historical material used in this chapter, is based upon Noam Even's research found in his unpublished Hebrew-language doctoral dissertation, "Civilian Casualties" (Bar-Ilan University, 2007).*

soldiers and three young civilians, a clear distinction was made between the two soldiers and the latter. The former were enshrined by the Defense Ministry's Office of Commemoration as "war casualties," while the other three were listed by the National Insurance Institute as "victims of hostile actions." In Haifa's official Remembrance Day commemoration ceremony a few months later, only the soldiers were mentioned. The families of the other three victims were deeply hurt.

The state has, since its very inception, sought to fittingly memorialize its war dead and support their surviving dependants. However, while the official focus in its first two decades was on those who died while serving their country as soldiers, questions concerning the increasing numbers of civilian casualties always hovered in the background. Was it right to ignore them and their families? Weren't they victims of the same enemy who chose to strike sometimes at military targets and other times at "softer" civilian populations? Could passive victims rightly be compared to soldiers who died defending others? But where did that leave soldiers killed in training accidents, or even off-duty? Did *they* rate the same honor as their comrades who fell in combat?

For a country founded in good part by old-school socialists, the ethos of universal equality was strong. However, early Israel society also loved its *sabra* ethic of warrior toughness. This view of the "New Hebrew Man" was part and parcel of the Zionist rejection of "old country" softness and accommodation. The state had such difficulty in acknowledging its less-macho diaspora roots that a memorial day for Holocaust victims was only established in conjunction with a commemoration of the Warsaw Ghetto Uprising. The government did not want too much attention paid to those who meekly went like "lambs to the slaughter" – even if they were innocent children.

Things would begin to change after the Six Day War. Smarting from their disastrous conventional military defeat and loss of territory, Israel's enemies began to increase their attacks on civilian targets—both in Israel and without. As Arab terror grew in the post-1967 era, growing numbers of civilian casualties compelled the state to address the very real needs of their surviving families. By 1970, in time for the spike in terror aimed at Israeli civilians from Munich to Ma'alot, the Victims of Enemy Actions Compensation Law was enacted. This law entitled terror victims to the same benefits that had been extended by the state to widows and orphans of IDF soldiers and was intended to help them move on with their lives. However, these victims were not officially *commemorated* by the state until much later.

Over the ensuing years, Israeli society began to change drastically—both politically and socially: The Labor Party-Histadrut (Workers Union) monopoly on governance ended with Menachem Begin's election in 1977; the Eighties found the country embroiled in the Lebanon War—the first war which actually fostered social divisiveness; the founders' socialist ethos began to slip away as the economy grew in leaps and bounds, and personal interests replaced the ideal of sacrifice for the common good. Living here since 1984, I have watched Israel's metamorphosis from quaint provinciality to broad-shouldered assertiveness, increasingly Western in feel and outlook.

The changes were also felt in the realm of commemoration. Menachem Begin's government began a project to identify hundreds of fighters killed in the pre-state period. The parents of soldiers killed in Lebanon began to request more personalized inscriptions on their children's gravestones. Most importantly, in 1997, a grassroots movement began to push for government recognition of terror victims on a par with her fallen soldiers.

A small group of bereaved parents established an organization which would become recognized as the "official representative" of terror victims—*Irgun Nifga'ay Pe'ulot Evah* (The Terror Victims Association). With the help of then-President Ezer Weizman, they succeeded in placing an official memorial to the victims of terror at the very epicenter of state commemoration— on Mt. Herzl, the site of Israel's main military cemetery and the final resting place of many of her leading statesmen. Their success, as historian and archivist Noam Even has described, was due in part to their timing. Their efforts coincided with Israel's Jubilee Year preparations and with a mounting wave of Arab terror that, in the wake of the Oslo accords, was hitting at Israel's soft underbelly in Tel Aviv and other cities. A monument (to which the names of all terror victims would be added once the necessary historic research was completed) was built and unveiled as part of Remembrance Day in Israel's Jubilee Year.

This notable accomplishment, however, was accompanied by a hard-fought battle. Those who represented the widows and families of IDF casualties, argued in Knesset committee meetings, in the media, and in a lawsuit brought against the government that such recognition—and in of all places, Mt. Herzl!—was an affront to their loss. Their basic argument was expressed by a war widow who questioned, "How could it be possible to compare our casualties with someone who died in a coffee house?!" Soldiers had given their lives defending others, they had been the people's emissaries who knowingly placed themselves in harm's way, and had sacrificed themselves for the state. Their memories deserved better than to be compared with someone who had the bad luck to be in the wrong place at the wrong time. One widow of a famous war hero even petitioned to have a physical barrier erected between her late husband's grave and the new monument!

Acrimonious debate continued in a special government committee (the Maltz Commission) established in 1999 to weigh the delicate questions surrounding the inclusion of terror victims in state memorials. Representatives of these victims argued that "their dead" were killed by the very same enemies, in the very same continuous warfare against the same small state that had taken the lives of so many soldiers. They weren't just "unlucky," they too were war dead—part and parcel of Israel's historic struggle for survival in the sea of hatred she still inhabits. They too had the right, as one widow put it, "to be part of our memory." Some also questioned the wisdom of grading victims, hinting that perhaps soldiers who died in accidents might also then occupy a different memorial space than those who fell in actual combat.

A year later, in a close vote of 9 to 7, the call for inclusion and the parity of pain won out. It was decided that Israel's Remembrance Day for the Fallen in Israel's Wars would also serve as the central day for memorializing "victims of enemy acts" and the day's official name was soon changed to reflect this. In something of a compromise, though, it was decided that a separate official ceremony to commemorate terror victims would be held at Mt. Herzl two hours after the annual ceremony in memory of fallen soldiers.

More recently, the three fathers whose children were killed in the aforementioned Haifa bus attack, won their struggle for their children's names to be included among their city's war dead.

Now these youths are mentioned in Haifa's official Remembrance Day ceremonies.

In response to the calls for inclusion by the families of terror victims, another bereaved father (a representative of Yad LaBanim, the official organization for memorializing IDF casualties) attempted to explain that the difference between soldiers and citizens was not a matter of parsing pain or memory, but of "legacy." For him, fallen soldiers teach about sacrifice for the common good, something which the state needs to perpetuate. It is the state's responsibility and in its interest to foster this selfless ethos.

> *So there is Holocaust Remembrance Day, which is a day in which we remember all the victims, but we don't speak of it as a legacy, and encourage them to be burned in the crematoria in Germany or Poland. ... I don't think that parents of terror victims want to wish our youth to follow in their children's footsteps. They [the terror victims] are victims of the fact that there is a conflict, victims of the fact that they are Jewish, that they are citizens in the State of Israel.... (Yoske Harari, in an interview with Jerusalem Post correspondent Aryeh Dean Cohen).*

One can hear clear echoes of the state's early struggles with the Shoah in this parent's argument—passive victims do not belong beside the new Jewish warriors. No thought is given to different types of "heroism." What about those who kept their faith even when all seemed lost? Or those like Janusz Korczak, the educator who accompanied his pupils into the gas chambers, staying with them until the very end? Or those who, despite facing the inhuman, kept a measure of human dignity themselves? I know that Harari and others want to point out that it is *just the way that they died* which separates these from those. But in equating legacy with death itself, in focusing solely on how soldiers met their end rather than on how they lived their lives, perhaps we lose the opportunity to learn something else.

When a life is tragically cut short, there is a tendency to look for meaning in the death itself. This makes it all too easy to turn ordinary people into heroes. But every life contains its own measure of meaning—in the deeds done, the relationships created. Isn't the way in which my son devoted himself to his studies day and night worthy of emulation? Isn't his visiting the hospitalized to raise the spirits of the bedridden deserving of notice? What about the time he gave his ice cream cone to his younger sister after hers had fallen to the ground? Isn't that, in its own small way, legacy enough to be remembered? Yet civic remembrance isn't aimed at the ordinary, is it?

This struggle for memory's place in the public sphere is by no means simple. A neighbor of mine lost a son who fell while fighting an attacking Arab force on Israel's border some years ago. Before the opening of our local annual memorial ceremonies last year, he bemoaned the focus on the survivors, on the bereaved, who are pitied for their loss. He argued that we, the bereaved, should be secondary to the memories of the fallen themselves. The day should be devoted to them—the heroes—and not to us, the victims of circumstance. I wondered whether he would have grouped our two sons together as heroes or not.

And yet, much of the tension that the fathers from Haifa experienced seems to have skipped over the communities of Judea and Samaria. Unfortunately, we have all been to too many funerals of friends, neighbors, or students for us to draw a line (whether warranted or not) between those killed while in uniform and those killed while playing hooky from grade school. The cumulative awareness of loss makes it difficult to go over specifics with a fine-tooth comb. Moreover, we, perhaps more than urbanites who have little daily contact with young combat soldiers, feel that we are all in this together. Jeeps enter our towns laden with dirty soldiers on a short break from patrol, hungry for a pizza or a hamburger. Not infrequently, by the time their order arrives, someone else has paid their bill. In smaller settlements, soldiers doing a stint of guard duty are offered home hospitality by the people they are guarding. Ideologically, we also feel united in the struggle against the same enemy who would just as readily shoot a baby in her mother's arms as attack a soldier at his post.

So, when the too-long list of names is read off on Remembrance Day in my local cemetery, nobody whose life has been taken by our enemies is left out. Soldier and citizen; fighter and student; young and old; hero or not.

CHAPTER TWELVE:
A DAY TO REMEMBER

*If there is one word that defines the fragility, the vulnerability
but also the invincibility of the human condition, it is memory.*

ELIE WEISEL, *ETHICS AND MEMORY*

The Jewish calendar moves through the lunar year from one
celebration to the next. As my family and I made it through
Purim and Passover still reeling from my son's murder, we reached
a period which marks one of the stronger demarcations between
Israeli culture and global Jewish life—the unique juxtaposition of
Remembrance Day and Independence Day.

Growing up in suburban Long Island in the Seventies meant that
American Memorial Day was just another one of several long
weekends that put off school or work until Tuesday. In mainstream
(that is Jewish, non-haredi) Israeli culture, Remembrance Day
is unlike anything else. To paraphrase a mishnah, "One who
has not seen Israeli Remembrance Day, has never seen public
commemoration in his life." It is, to most Israelis, sacred. All
public frivolity is canceled, the media devotes its air time and
printed pages to remembering the fallen, and somber gatherings are
held throughout the entire nation—in city concert halls and town

gymnasiums—at precisely eight o'clock in the evening. The next morning, at precisely 11:00 am, sirens sound throughout the country and people stop whatever they are doing, even driving on the highways, to stand in silence for two minutes to honor those killed while serving in the IDF and civilians murdered by terrorists.

A week before Remembrance Day, we were visited by a pair of high school students. They brought us an official invitation to the main memorial ceremony and a single flower. I had never, in my ten years in Efrat, attended this ceremony. One of the teenagers also asked that I speak briefly, as a representative of the bereaved families. The ceremony was to be held in the town gymnasium—Efrat's largest indoor public space. Beforehand, there would be a gathering of Efrat's bereaved families in the adjacent library. There, we would hear from some high school students who have spent the past few weeks filming interviews with local families who have lost a loved one in IDF service or to terrorism.

I miss this discussion as I need to first attend afternoon prayers—held half an hour before sunset. Afterwards, as I make my way to the library, I bump into Rabbi Riskin, our town's Chief Rabbi, who is also on his way to this pre-ceremony meeting. It is the period between Passover and Shavuot known as *Sfirat Ha'omer* and the rabbi, usually clean shaven, has a few weeks stubble on his cheeks. In another day, in celebration of Israel's independence, he will shave this off. We look at each other a bit oddly, tears welling in the eyes of both—knowing that I am among the newest members of this exclusive group; knowing that there is nothing to say. It is odd walking into the room to join some of my neighbors marked by similar loss. I am the new initiate joining this circle of grief for the first time. The newest member of a club which no one wishes to join.

After this initial meeting, we are escorted by high school students out of the library and led the twenty meters to the community center where my wife and I pick up our two girls who have been brought over by their baby-sitter. There, in the entrance foyer, pictures of the dead have been posted on dark construction paper and in front of each face is a memorial candle waiting to be lit. My son Elisha Dan is with his mother in Jerusalem and I help my daughters light the flame. Our teenage companions, whose attention makes us feel like porcelain dignitaries—fragile VIPs who may break apart at any moment—lead us down the stairs to the gym floor.

The bleachers, holding hundreds of people, are full. On the floor itself, another hundred or so plastic chairs have been set up in front of a screen and stage. We have orchestra seats. The ceremony begins with the lowering of the flag to half-mast. Three soldiers stand at attention while the Israeli version of "Taps" is played. Then, a two minute siren sounds. Everyone in the packed hall stands at attention in complete silence.

The program on the stage has been created by our town's youth groups and the educational staff of the local army base, just two miles down the road. There are dramatic readings, sad songs sung by teenagers, a short play, a speech by Rabbi Riskin and another by our mayor. The evening is serious and somber. When it is my turn to speak, I mount the steps to the podium, the harsh lights hurting my eyes. I begin to read:

> *"Happy families are all alike; sad families are each sad in their own way." Thus Tolstoy opened his famous work, Anna Karenina. Sadness has its own deep loneliness. Every family struggles in its own way. Although I was asked by this evening's organizers to represent the*

137

families of the deceased, I have no presumptions that I can represent anyone. All I can do is present my own private sadness and pain.

What can I say? Remembrance Day is usually devoted to the memory of those war heroes who fell in combat fighting for our land and nation. Soldiers who gave their lives for their country. They fought for us, the living, and we are here today, able to recall their deeds, only on account of their heroism.

What, I ask myself, what did my son, only 16-years-old, who was murdered in a library and not on the battlefield, what did his death give us? He never leapt on a grenade to save his company; he never risked his life storming the enemy. He died holding a holy book, not a rifle.

I am only a bereaved father; a father who has lost his beloved son. It is difficult for me to speak of this loss from a place beyond my own pain – in fact, it is difficult to venture beyond the unique intimacy of my own private pain. However, I realize that his death, together with that of the other students in Mercaz HaRav, holds something beyond my own suffering.

My son never saved anyone, but perhaps this evening it is worthwhile to recall that the cruel attack in Mercaz HaRav reminded us, the nation of Israel, that we are no ordinary nation. Yes, we are a people—as nation that dwells alone, suffering terrors, but still surviving – but we are more than just a nation. We are also a more intimate group, we are a family. "We are brothers, sons of one man" (Genesis 42:13) – we are not just the People of Israel, but also the Sons of Jacob.

The responses to this massacre, both here and overseas, were not the responses of just a nation bound together by geography, language, or heritage. The way that Jews the world over felt violated, the prayers and help offered by so many, these were more the responses of a family in mourning—like the tears that our Matriarch Rahel cries for her children. The horrible death of these yeshivah students—so young and so innocent—touched something deep in the hearts of so many Jews. It reached a place that only a death in the family can.

I will never forget the way that Rabbi Weiss hugged me close when he gave me the still nearly unbelievable news. But, since then, my family and I have been embraced by our friends, especially those in Efrat, like members of one family. People cooked for us, prayed with us, worried about us. The solitude of loss is difficult. And, perhaps as an immigrant who left his family behind to come home to Israel many years ago, more difficult still. However, I learned, and it seems to me that the Jewish people remembered—during a time too dark to properly describe—that "we are brothers."

My brothers, people of Efrat, today much is made of the "family of the bereaved." But today is also a day to recall the larger family—the family that is our people. True, when we disagree with each other, we do have the tendency to fight like only family can—but in our better moments, we can also love each other like family. "We are brothers, sons of one man." The same man, Jacob, who succeeded in winning God's blessing only when he kept his own voice, but adopted the hands of Esav. We saw this too in Mercaz HaRav. We saw who was willing to put his own life on the line and go after the terrorist. Captain David Shapiro—a religious soldier, grasping in one hand the sword, the other clasping the holy books of our faith. The sword and the book—this is the way of Gush Etzion and Efrat.

There is nothing more private than deep sadness—a sadness that rises up like waters of the deep in moments like these. However, memory and memorial are also public. We come together this evening to mourn the loss of our fallen sons. Each one is a family member whose place at the table remains empty. Rahel, our mother, who died on the road to Efrat, cries for all her children. And we, who today make Efrat our home, cry for all of ours.

Upon finishing, as I turn to leave the stage, I look into the faces of the teenagers who have organized this ceremony. They are crying. I am too. I make my way back to my seat and my daughter climbs on my lap to bury her face in my chest so that she too can cry.

A year later, I learn that my speech, traveling as words will over the internet, has made its way into a number of far afield high school Remembrance Day programs. Another chance for tears.

CHAPTER THIRTEEN:
VICTIM'S VACATION

The suffering of the many is partial condolence.

HEBREW FOLK EXPRESSION

Those who have experienced tragedy, either directly or as witnesses, often feel compelled to turn their shock, pain, and/or outrage into something positive. Doing some good is a way to counterbalance the bad to which they have been exposed. Israelis have suffered through years of terror and major wars which have left scars on nearly every household. Unlike other places further removed from the line of fire, here, everyone knows someone who has lost a loved one to the Arabs' refusal to accept a Jewish political presence in the Middle East. And unlike other places, Israel is blessed with an abundance of truly righteous people who turn to those hurt by war and terror with an outstretched hand offering aid of all sorts. There's "Camp Koby," "One Family" and hosts of smaller groups doing what they can.

Some months after my son's murder, I received an invitation to attend a weekend for bereaved families run by a small organization which I had never heard of before. (For the sake of other participants' privacy, this group will remain anonymous). The letter described two-and-a-half days of activities—arts and crafts, nature trips, drama—all connected to loss. The weekend's theme was "dreams" and would feature a facilitator who taught psychodrama therapy. Something about it sounded intriguing, but I was hesitant to commit my family to the kindness of strangers in the isolated hotel where the weekend was to take place. A local rabbi I knew was listed as the weekend's "spiritual coordinator" and he encouraged me to come, assuring me that the organizers not only meant well, but actually knew how to translate that into the little things, like child care and Shabbat observance. At the least, I figured that the weekend wouldn't be a survival test of trying to entertain bored kids while holed up in a noisy hotel.

A few weeks later, we packed the car and set off, northward bound, not knowing exactly what to expect, but cautiously hopeful that spending a few days in the company of other bereaved families might somehow help lift the heavy weight of loss which my wife and I still felt all too often. We arrived at the modest hotel after the usual fun of family car travel with three children in the backseat, well ready for a break. We were relieved that the younger kids were whisked away by some dedicated teenagers who had been hired to babysit, while my son joined a group activity for older children. Before dinner, there was painting for the adults and afterwards a drumming workshop. The next day we went as a group to an outdoor recreation site for a short nature walk and some other activities.

Much of what was offered was typical of the good, clean family fun available at any number of Israeli guest houses at which we have vacationed over the years. Of course, the difference here was that you knew that you and everyone else painting, drumming, or listening to the tour guide had some terrible secret in their past which had brought them to this weekend. "And who did you lose?" was the question that floated just beneath our friendly small talk over meals. There were many parents of dead children—some killed in infancy by terrorists, some as soldiers in battle. My wife chatted with a young mother of two boys whose husband had stayed behind to work in his factory during the Second Lebanon War while she and the children traveled south to safety. He died trying to make it to a bomb shelter during a Hezbullah barrage.

We were rookies—still in our first year of mourning. Some offered us advice about how to run the annual memorial evenings. Others gasped when we told them who we were. The Mercaz massacre still commanded more attention than nearly any other terrorist attack had for quite some time. Even here, my wife and I joked, we had a measure of celebrity.

From what I could see, some participants had moved well past their loss, but still enjoyed these retreats with the friends they had made in these therapeutic meetings over the years. For others, though, these weekends were the only bit of light in lives that had been crushed by despair and pain. One older woman cried as she described losing her son and then getting divorced in the aftermath, leaving her all alone now for many years. As she held her head in her hands, the image that she conjured in my mind was of a pile of human dust, something ground down to bits. Her life, as she told it, was divided into the time "before my tragedy" and "after my tragedy". I wondered if I would also come to count the days like her.

Much of our time was spent in a type of group therapy featuring the psychodramatization of dreams. The facilitator had brought along a married pair of his students to help with this. He was the director, they were the actors. The three of them, with the group's participation, staged a number of participants' dreams. Seeing one's dream acted out allowed for a measure of actualization and even for a re-scripting of thoughts, fears, and wishes.

One mother had a nightmare in which her dead son passed by her on a crowded train and try as she might, she just couldn't reach him. With the group's help, she recreated the scene so that she could once again hold him in her arms. Another woman wanted to confront her overbearing father who had favored her prettier and slimmer sisters over the years. Yet another re-enacted a recurring nightmare of being chased by a mysterious stranger. The acting was wisely halted as it became clearer that this stranger might not in fact be a stranger, but someone the woman had known quite well as a young girl and the dream was beginning to resemble an actual, but repressed, scene of family violence or worse. On a lighter note, my wife brought the house down as she reenacted her ongoing, but unsuccessful, attempts to learn to drive in Israel.

Overall, the weekend was an enjoyable change of pace. This was, on a certain level, quite odd. We had spent our time in a cross-section of Israeli society—with religious and secular, old and young, physicists and housewives—an almost random group whose common denominator was having lost someone to a violent, politically-motivated death. It was like traveling through a looking glass into a parallel world—a world which was normal in every way, except for one thing.... Is this what meetings of

Shoah survivors are like? I wondered if the rest of my life would revolve around such groups like some of the others whom we had met. Was this something positive, to be encouraged, or was it a measure of dysfunction? Would we ever again be normal? Or would we keep seeking out others who carried the same brand of pain that had been so recently seared into our own flesh?

CHAPTER FOURTEEN:
MANIPULATION OF MEMORY

All I have is a voice
To undo the folded lie…

W. H. AUDEN, "SEPTEMBER 1, 1939"

T he parents who lost children at Mercaz HaRav (with the
exception of the Maharatahs) are gathered together in the
Cohens' home. The Cohens are the parents of the youngest victim,
the class clown, Neriah. They live in Jerusalem's Old City and
are part of a small group of Jews dedicated to reinhabiting areas
of the walled city that were abandoned by Jews during the lethal
Arab riots of the 1930's. Their home, in the area designated as
the "Moslem Quarter" under the British Mandate, is reached by
walking through twisting narrow alleys of Jerusalem stone. We
are accompanied by a pair of armed young men whose job it is to
shuttle visitors and residents safely from the Western Wall area to
the Jewish homes nestled between Arab ones.

Like nearly all the inhabitants of the Old City—Jewish, Moslem
or Christian—the Cohens try to live a modern life within the
confines of medieval architecture. Space is a scarce commodity.
Their home is a collection of hallways, passages, and stairs

connecting numerous small rooms. We walk down a narrow hall to enter the combination living room-dining room. Most of this little room is situated under a metal loft and the resulting low ceiling creates a hobbit-like atmosphere that borders between cozy and cramped.

We sit down at the Cohens' dining room table which, like mine, is flanked by a picture of a murdered son. This is the first time that we, the families of these murdered youths, are meeting outside of any specific "event." There is small talk, food is passed and we ask Yitzhak and his wife about life deep within the alleys of the Old City. But this is not a social meeting. There is a reason we have all been called together.

A middle-aged man joins us. He is carrying a collection of maps, documents and architectural drawings. Rolling them out, he begins to describe a large-scale project intertwined with his sad life story. His brother was murdered by terrorists. For years he has been trying to advance his plans for a fitting memorial—a promenade overlooking biblical Nabulus, called *Shekhem* in Hebrew. He explains that the military powers-that-be like the plan. The construction of a promenade connecting biblical Joseph's Tomb with the bypass road to the Jewish settlements while skirting the Arab city of Shekhem will mean less friction between Jews and Arabs in the region. (The irony of this explanation, delivered while we sit in a home surrounded by Arab Moslems, makes me smile.) This is a multi-million dollar undertaking upon which the bereaved man has spent years of his life; years, it seems, that have taken their toll on him. Since his brother's death he has moved from place to place and gotten divorced, all while unsuccessfully trying to market his memorial plan. To me, he cuts a tragic figure, bereft of nearly everything but the hope that his project can now be invigorated.

And that is where we, the "Mercaz families", come in. He wants to add our sons' names to the project. By expanding the memorial aspect of his plan to include us, he knows that he has a better chance of moving it forward. Bereaved parents in Israel, whether their children were killed while serving in the IDF or by terrorists, benefit from a "halo effect." Like ball-players pitching used cars, they are more likely to be trusted, to be listened to. Bereaved parents have sacrificed for the country. Perhaps due to survivor's guilt, they are granted a mysterious, nearly moral, authority which makes it difficult to say no to them.

A true life example: I was once late getting my daughters to an activity organized by a group for bereaved siblings. A traffic cop wasn't allowing cars, including the cab in which we sat, to turn in the direction we were headed. I told our driver, "One minute," got out of the car and told the officer that I had lost my son at Mercaz HaRav and explained where we were going. Without a word, she let us through. As I returned to the taxi, our cabby looked at me in amazement, wondering what in the world I could have whispered to the tough-looking policewoman that got her to change her mind.

The man proposing the Shekhem promenade knew that we, the newly minted bereaved, could gain access to government offices, help raise funds and get media attention for his stalled project in ways that no one else could. Perhaps it was difficult for him to sacrifice the singularity of a memorial built exclusively for his brother, but better to share the wealth than have none.

As he wound up his pitch, we all sat in shocked silence for a moment. I think that we knew, on one level or another, that we possessed a measure of newfound cultural capital (or macabre celebrity) since our sons had been killed. But, I think this was also the first time for all us that we were confronted by so blatant a request to exploit it. This project, whatever its merits, had nothing to do with *our* children—who they were, where they lived, what they studied. The total lack of subtlety—the sorry, desperate pitch—was a like a slap in the face. Everyone politely thanked him and slightly embarrassed, purposefully vague promises were made to be in touch.

After he left, our host began his own pitch. Together with my ex-wife's husband, David Moriah (Rivkah hadn't come this evening), Yitshak Cohen proceeded to lay out a plan to capitalize on our unenviable, but unarguable, status as bereaved families. The idea was to form a type of social-cum-political action committee. As such, we would be able to promulgate press releases on the issues of the day, raise money for a variety of worthwhile projects and ultimately try to influence our country's agenda like any of the other myriad lobbyists who compete for the public's attention. (Of course, it went without saying that we would be propounding a religious, right-wing point of view, acting as a counterbalance to the secular, left-wing slant of Israel's dominant elite.)

David expounded upon the media's unfairness, on how other groups had exploited the public's sympathy and how, here we were now with the opportunity to do the same but for the greater good. Here was our chance! He told us that an organization that collected money for various Israel charities (and was also helping Yashlatz to raise money) had volunteered to help our still-unborn organization as well. We would decide where and how to put this money to use. I could see the visions of dollars dancing in his head as he described the enormous potential: American Jewry so much wanted to do something, they were just waiting for the go-ahead to shower us with funds. His wife, Avraham David's mother, had already been flown to Staten Island by one American chronic fundraiser to share her story at a charity barbeque event. What in the world were we waiting for?!

I felt like someone had kicked me in the stomach. I knew that the Cohens had chosen, by deciding to live where they did—amongst Moslems who felt that they had no right to be there—to lead a politically charged life. They were part of a project which (in many ways similar to the entire State of Israel) was cheered by some and reviled by many. They needed a certain amount of political-cum-public opinion buoyancy to stay afloat in the choppy waters of one of the most contested and congested areas in the Middle East. But David? For me the notion of so blatantly institutionalizing the exploitation of tragedy was disgusting. It reeked of cheapening my son's memory, of prostituting our pain in a sickeningly vulgar fashion. I was livid. I was also determined that this plan, no matter what, would not see the light of day. I took a silent oath in my mind, "This will not come to pass."

The families began an animated discussion over the proposal. I argued that yes, the media pays attention to the bereaved, yes a newspaper will be more willing to print an op-ed berating the coddling of terrorists by someone who has himself suffered a loss, but in the end—they are only after a story to sell to their audience, nothing more, nothing less. It was wishful thinking to imagine that any group we might evolve into would really be able to make much of a difference by grabbing headlines. At the time, the fate of two IDF soldiers, kidnapped by Hezbollah in Lebanon, was being addressed almost daily in the press. One of them was "lucky" to have an attractive, articulate wife. I argued that it was this fact, as much as any other concerns, that kept their tragic story on the front pages—pretty, concerned Karnit Goldwasser sold newspapers.

151

As we argued back and forth, some of the parents in favor, some against, the level of tension in the small room rose. In atypical Israeli fashion, the debate was fairly level-headed. We all knew that each of us was still deeply mourning our loss; we were aware of each other's fragility. But despite the efforts taken not to offend, there was a push to move things to a vote. This raised the tension even more. Voting meant taking a definite stand against those who voted the other way. We were really only a group by dint of a terrible shared fate. We were only bound together by the solidarity of joint loss. The very act of voting, of turning this delicate bond into something so coarsely quantifiable, would rip apart the tenuous ties that held us together. The act of voting, it seemed to me, was a reflection in miniature of what those pushing for "organizing" sought to do—to remake the sadness of loss into a material tool. A vote, in and of itself, would give the appearance that some new and binding framework had been created. But I wondered why on earth any of us not interested in this would actually go along. There was no real authority here, no power to censure anyone.

I had kept what I thought of as my big guns in abeyance, hoping not to have to use them. But, as Yitshak pushed for a vote, I prepared to tell everyone that I was going to fight against anything that any so-called representative group created tonight was going to do. Not in my name, and not in my son's memory, would money be raised, press releases sent out, agendas and ambitions fulfilled. I was getting ready to tell them that if they thought they had a hook into press coverage, imagine the waves that the angry father fighting *against* the exploitation of his son's memory would make. They would not be able to make a move that I would not counter with my own phone calls to the radio, my own op-eds. Whatever story they had to sell, I could guarantee them that covering the more colorful infighting among the "Mercaz families" would be too appealing for the media to resist. I mentally girded my loins and prepared for battle. But I didn't have to say a word.

One of the other fathers spoke instead. He said that he felt political activities were not proper during the first year of mourning our children's death. Quietly, in a few sentences, he spoke of the value of educational activities—talking in schools, at memorial ceremonies—but he stressed that the realm of politics was far removed from the appropriate perpetuation of our children's memories—during this, the first year after their murder. By emphasizing the message "it's too soon" he was able to gently push away the call for organizing without attacking the idea itself. It provided a way out for everybody, even though it was clear that by not acting now, while the memory of this horrific attack was still fresh in the public's mind, no organization would ever emerge.

No votes were cast. There would be no marketing of our pain. My son's memory would remain untainted by the commercialization of grief. And we, the families of the Mercaz HaRav massacre, were able to depart the Old City cordially, keep our fellowship of sorrow intact for another day.

CHAPTER FIFTEEN:
ISRAELI MOURNING

Either fellowship or death.

On a mild and sunny winter's day, I leave home early in the morning to make my way to the small campus of an Israeli kibbutz college. This collection of classrooms, park benches, and an auditorium or two is located in Ramat Efal, not far from Tel Aviv. I am on my way to attend a conference on mourning in Israeli culture. It is sponsored by the kibbutz movement's academic wing and two pluralistic centers for the study of Jewish texts and traditions. (These study centers have become increasingly popular over the last decade, as secular Israelis have looked for ways to study Judaism without giving themselves over to Orthodoxy.) The day's program consists of a few panel discussions interspersed with smaller workshops. The speakers include academics, journalists and a rabbi or two. The audience is nearly all female; most are social workers.

As an immigrant who lives most of his life surrounded by religious Jews, I am always interested in hearing what the "the other half" (secular and Israeli) has to say. Among the mostly secular women,

I, with my beard, larger than average yarmulka, and *tsitsit* (ritual fringes) hanging below my belt, am easily identifiable as something other than your average kibbutz seminar participant.

These secular Israelis are happy to talk to me about how their socialist forefathers sought to secularize their Jewish heritage. These pioneers looked for ways to use the holy tongue for the most mundane of purposes. In large part, they succeeded, lifting conceits from holy texts to express their own earthly longings. Secular Israeli culture is a fascinating mix of the Jewishly-oriented with the tradition-alienated, the Middle Eastern shuk with the Polish shtetl. It has a vibrancy unlike anything found anywhere else. The most trivial conversations echo the language of the Prophets, youngsters flirt near Second Temple relics, and weekly television shows, broadcast on the Sabbath in utter disregard of Jewish law, feature discussions of that week's Torah reading.

I sit through the day listening to the participants discuss various aspects of mourning. Some address public concerns; some, more private ones. One of the threads that runs through many of the discussions is a certain amount of discomfort with the traditional expectations of Jewish mourning. The austerity of the plain burial shroud which covers the deceased (with few exceptions, no casket is used), the lack of flowers, the absence of music, the Aramaic prayers—these combine to give a traditional funeral a certain religious severity which is quite foreign to secular Israelis. Since interment in Israel is handled for the most part by Haredi-run municipal burial societies whose cultural distance from the average secular Israeli is quite pronounced, the tail-end of the life cycle can be somewhat alienating.

The challenges of mourning rituals for the secular were addressed by several of the speakers. Some told tales of actual battles between family members of the deceased: secular kibbutzniks fought with religious relatives over whether *kaddish* would be said over the grave. Some described generational tensions over the meaning of mourning within the kibbutz—was it a time for earnest discussion or for listening to pop music? Others discussed the search for alternative rituals reflective of secular, rather than religious values. Why, at the end of a life in which the divine was consistently ignored should God suddenly get to play such a major role?

I listened to these complaints with both interest and a certain degree of equanimity. For me, the religious aspects (and yes, demands) of Jewish life and death were anything but disturbing. They were as comfortably familiar, and often as invigorating, as fresh snow for a Laplander. But, I could appreciate their strangeness for one raised in the temperate climes of Israeli secularity.

One of the last speakers was an Israeli Reform rabbi, originally from the Former Soviet Union. He spoke of the difficulties that FSU immigrants faced in adapting to Israeli life—and with it, Israeli death. There were infrequent but difficult cases of young soldiers killed in action who were not Jewish. Their burial in regular IDF, that is, Jewish, cemeteries was halakhically problematic. Although the previous Chief Rabbi, Rav Bakshi Doron, had arrived at a reasonable solution that left nearly everyone satisfied, the mention of these cases still served to rouse the ire of secularists who saw them as yet another example of halakhic stubbornness.

More to the point, though, was his description of these immigrants' unease with religious customs that are foreign to them. In the FSU, floral arrangements and graveside music were the norm. In Israel, the spartan Jewish rituals they were encountering for the first time seemed almost disrespectful to them. Most difficult of all, though, was the isolation that sitting *shivah* entailed for many immigrants with little or no family in the country. Instructed by their local burial society to stay at home during mourning, most lacked the dozens of relatives and friends that Israelis usually have to sit with them through their loss. Nobody was there to feed them, hold their hand or offer a shoulder upon which to cry as they spent the week of mourning alone with only their sorrow for company.

As I listened to him, I couldn't help but reflect upon my own situation as an immigrant. Mourning as a practice takes place within community: the *minyan*, the synagogue, the neighborhood. While pain is personal and loss itself is not easily shared, the wisdom of tradition has prescribed community contact and not isolation for the mourner. Yet this begs the question—from where does community spring? As a religious Jew, and an immigrant who left the land of his birth behind years ago, I would answer that it stems from mutual commitment. Community is not an extension of friendship (although you may have friends in your community), nor is it necessarily a derivative of larger social groupings like nations, for it may in fact cross over borders and extend beyond nationalities. Rather a community is a group bound by a common cause which requires the group's members for its successful accomplishment.

An orchestra is a good example. In order to play a given piece of music, each member does his part and contributes to the production as a whole. The players are bound to the score, and through it, to each other. In addition to members' different skill levels, it is easy to imagine that some members hold different levels of commitment to the making of music than others. Some may want to practice until perfection; others are content with a reasonable rendition requiring significantly less investment. The orchestra will only be able to perform together if its members can agree on what constitutes a suitable outcome. Without a common goal, there is no reason for the group to stay united and so the community naturally withers and dies.

Community, then, is goal-driven (although goals can range from the ridiculous to the sublime). Its members need each other to attain their mutual goal. Jewish religious life creates community through its demands on the individual, which cannot be accomplished alone. Some *mitsvot* explicitly require a quorum, while others demand specialized skills—like ritual slaughter or blowing a shofar—which relatively few possess, thus encouraging coalescence into collectives to more readily fulfill these commandments. Bound together to do God's will as outlined in our Torah and understood by our Sages, we pray, study, visit the sick, feed the needy, and sometimes argue—together, as a community. It is within this community, too, that the joys and pains of life and death are shared.

It was into an overcrowded, overflowing synagogue that I walked the Friday evening after burying my son. I could hear the singing of the *Kabbalat Shabbat* prayers from my home before I entered. People were praying together, their voices lifted in song, with a fervor well beyond that of an ordinary Friday night. My neighbors—some friends and some the merest of acquaintances— my community, reeling from the previous day's events, needed each other. They needed to lend their voices, hopes, thanks, and prayers to each other—each voice supporting his fellow's in turning to God. It was this need that brought them, and me, together in worship and in mutual aid. It was my turn this time; another time it might be somebody else's.

Those lacking community lose doubly, for unshared joy is lessened and unshared pain sharpened. I am grateful for my community and I feel for these FSU immigrants; their plight deserves attention. But, as a practicing Jew I believe, that what is needed is not less obligation, but more community. The relationship between the two is linear, not inverse: stronger commitment generally leads to stronger community.

A year later, on another Friday night, on the eve of the first anniversary of my son's murder, I gave the evening's sermon on the week's Torah reading. Our custom is to rotate this duty among our members. The week's Torah reading was *Mishpatim*, literally *Laws*. It is devoted almost entirely to iconic "Old Testament" rules and regulations: you shall do this, you shall not do not this. I pointed out the need for societal rules and how fortunate we were to have a God-centered set. Following the philosopher Levinas, I spoke of the differences between the ethical and the political. The former takes place between two individuals; the latter is what is required to facilitate our dealings with each other in the larger grouping of the *polis* (or community). The Torah's laws are aimed at both.

The body of my short talk is not important. But what I said was meant to express recognition of and gratitude for those who stood by me as I recited *kaddish*; those who prepared food for my mourning family; those who invited my too-young-to-sit-*shivah* daughters to play at their homes while their parents cried. I discussed the importance of community and concluded by quoting Margaret Mead, "It takes a village to raise a child." I told the assembled that the same is needed to bury one. It takes a community. I was, and am, lucky to be part of one.

CHAPTER SIXTEEN:
APPROPRIATION OF DEATH

It is forbidden to derive benefit from a cadaver.

BABYLONIAN TALMUD, AVODAH ZARA 29b

There is no stopping time. Month after month passed and the last of the Hebrew months, Adar, was coming up. The first anniversary of my son's murder would soon arrive. On several occasions I had heard a rumor that a mysterious benefactor had decided to donate eight Torah scrolls in memory of the murdered youths and give one to each family. Like many other aspects of the year, this had the potential to be a bit more complicated for our family—split as we are into the Moses and Moriah clans.

As the date of the massacre's anniversary drew closer, we were informed that the rumor was true. In fact, not only was a scroll to be presented to each family, but this was to take place as part of a huge production, webcast live throughout the Jewish world. This event was billed as a "worldwide Torah installation and *siyum*" (completion of Torah study). It was meant to be something dramatic, something moving, something that would serve to connect the Jewish world to our sons' deaths. An entire organization, *B'Lev Echad* (With One Heart) was created to move this project forward. Its website described the motivation behind their initiative.

> *This horrific crime was more than an attack on one group of yeshivah talmidim [students]. It was an attack on the Torah itself....*
>
> *As the first yahrzeit [anniversary] approaches, men, women, and children are gathering to pay homage to the eight holy martyrs—eight living Sifrei Torah— whose hearts beat to the rhythm of the Torah and who perished with its holy words on their lips. By marking this occasion with public Torah learning, thousands of participants are uniting under the banner of the Torah, recognizing it as the ideal for which these young men lived their lives, and proclaiming it as the source of the Jew's unconquerable spirit.*

An admirable aim, requiring an investment of hundreds of hours of work and hundreds of thousands of dollars to implement. The logistics of getting eight scrolls written, a curriculum planned for eight days of study, 300 separate institutions involved, an original theme song written, a video highlighting Jewish unity produced, and transmitting the entire event live throughout the world were formidable. And somewhere in the rush, in the fog of organization, nobody remembered to ask the parents of the boys whose blood had stained the halls where this extravaganza was to take place, just what *they* thought of the idea.

I first got wind that something big was being planned about two months before the anniversary, after Rivkah Moriah returned from a Yashlatz fundraising trip to the U.S. where she had met with some of the B'Lev Echad people. She and her husband called a meeting of the families to discuss and coordinate the upcoming *yahrzeit.* She told us that she had met with some sort of committee that the donor had set up to organize the installation of the scrolls, but it seemed that neither she nor anybody else for that matter was too clear on what exactly was being planned. What she did have was the phone number of a Yeshivah University undergraduate student who was involved with B'Lev Echad as well as a surfeit of frustration (which would soon grow beyond that) with Mercaz HaRav.

First, some background: Mercaz HaRav was the first, and for many years the only, Zionist institution of higher Torah learning in Israel. The yeshivahs in Israel at that time were old school, Yiddish-speaking, institutions that sought to recreate an idealized version of the pre-Shoah European yeshivah milieu, including disengagement from the secular world that surrounded them. Mercaz HaRav, on the other hand, was meant from its inception to be something different. Its founder was Rabbi Avraham Yitzhak HaKohen Kook, Israel's first Chief Rabbi and one of the past century's most unique thinkers. Although himself a product of the Old World yeshivahs, he embraced the idea of political Zionism—the establishment of a Jewish state in the Holy Land— as the fruition not just of 2,000 years of diaspora dreams, but as the fullest expression of Judaism itself. This was a bold stance at a time when most political Zionists saw the Jewish religion as something to be overcome in the struggle to establish a state and many rabbis wanted little to do with the secular Zionist state and its earthly politics.

Rabbi Kook's yeshivah combined traditional Talmud study with the study of Bible and Jewish philosophy. Even more radically, the yeshivah espoused devotion to the Zionist cause (and then the state itself) which was viewed as ushering in a new age, the "flowering of our redemption." Rabbi Kook, much like his secular socialist contemporaries, was an earthly messianist—intent upon building the Jewish state as a step toward a better future for all mankind.

Mercaz HaRav flourished as an institution and came to represent a unique blend of Zionism and Torah, of mystical thought and Jewish law which spawned a generation of religious-Zionist institutions, thinkers, and leaders. Its own *roshei yeshivah* (deans) were some of the most important leaders in the religious-Zionist world and its students took their places as the leading lights of this small, but important sector of Israeli society.

Somewhere in the 1990's things changed. While once Mercaz HaRav had been the undisputed leading light of religious Zionism, its authoritative hold on the public began to slip. A plethora of competing religious Zionist institutions had sprung up, many headed by Mercaz HaRav graduates, and the yeshivah succumbed to in-house rivalry and leadership struggles, most notably the founding of a break-away institution headed by Rabbi Zvi Yehudah Tau. Ironically, the brutal massacre which took place in its library thrust Mercaz HaRav back into the spotlight it had once enjoyed.

The families of the massacre had been touched by the unfortunate institutional infighting as well (although until we met to discuss the *yahrzeit*, I was unaware of this). A grandfather of one of the murdered boys, a learned and well-respected rabbi, had been a teacher for many years at Mercaz HaRav. However, he had left with Rabbi Tau, and was, I learned, like the other so-called "rebels," a persona non grata in his old home. During the first Torah installation at Mercaz HaRav, a month after the massacre, words were exchanged between him and some strident Mercaz HaRav loyalists who still felt betrayed by the decade-old split. He was bluntly refused entry into the yeshivah—in spite of being there to mourn and honor his murdered grandson's memory. The boy's parents were understandably upset by this, but admirably kept so quiet about it that only those who witnessed the painful slight were aware that it had occurred.

Now, Rivkah had decided to devote herself to public relations (ie, fundraising) for Yashlatz, something which the high school had never pursued in its pre-massacre days. But it would have been impossible to expect any institution, and especially one as perpetually financially distressed as an Israeli yeshivah, to ignore the financial opportunities that the sympathy generated by the tragedy afforded. Even if its directors themselves were distraught at the horror behind all the attention (as they sincerely were), the publicity and public sympathy couldn't simply be dismissed when there were salaries to be paid, students to feed, and a building to maintain. I understood this and accepted it. I knew that my son, together with the other boys, would feature on any Yashlatz or Mercaz HaRav publicity material for some time.

I resigned myself to this inevitable capitalization of death. I knew that for Mercaz HaRav, this was going to be a chance to recapture some of its past glory; to return to the days when it was Israel's national yeshivah. I really didn't care. At least regarding Yashlatz, I felt that it was reasonable that those who wanted to spend their money on something in my son's memory could do so in a place where it might help to ease the pain of his surviving friends and classmates—but I really didn't want to be involved. My family in the U.S. had wanted to establish some type of memorial fund in my son's name, but I refused. Instead, I told them to direct memorial donations either to Yashlatz or other pre-existing organizations and leave me out of it. My wife, some PR-savvy neighbors, and my parents worked together to direct donors' money to the high school.

And now, months later, at this second meeting of the families, accusations of unfair competition in the race for donor money were being leveled by the Moriahs at Mercaz HaRav. They claimed that Yashlatz was being shunted aside by the older, more venerable institution with its greater name recognition. It was true that everyone in Israel had heard of Mercaz. After the massacre, many others had as well. But only those closely associated with the high school had any idea what "Yashlatz" was. It was true that there was confusion among the general public (and all the more so in the donor-rich overseas Jewish community) concerning the two institutions. While Yashlatz, the high school where my son studied, and Mercaz HaRav, the graduate yeshivah, shared parts of the same campus and each benefitted from the other's proximity in various ways—they were completely separate and independent entities, especially financially. However, many people, including some of Jerusalem's own politicians, assumed that they must be one bi-level institution. So it made sense that well-meaning donors who wanted to help the high school which had borne the brunt of the terrorist attack and whose dean had made a name for himself on Israeli prime time television, assumed that writing a check to "Yeshivat Mercaz HaRav" was the way to do this—even if it was not the case.

I didn't, and still don't know, whether accusations of spotlight grabbing and worse had any basis in fact. But, given the unfortunate and hurtful incident at Mercaz HaRav months earlier, and the Moriahs' angry insistence that Yashlatz was being short-changed and stiff-armed by her neighbor, it was not surprising that the plans for the gala memorial event, the "Worldwide Celebration of Jewish Unity", would generate a struggle over the appropriation of commemoration and even of death itself.

The B'Lev Echad organization was conceived by a wealthy American Jew who decided to donate one Torah scroll in memory of each of the slain youth. He wanted to mark the boys' death with some type of event which would span the diversity of the Jewish world. Unusually, he also decided to remain anonymous. He approached an industrious college undergraduate he knew and asked him to set up a committee to handle the gifting of these scrolls to the boys' families.

The committee met in the fall of 2008 and began to plan ways to reach out to hundreds of schools, communities and synagogues in order to involve them with an event aimed at helping Jews world over emerge from the darkness "by the light of *mitsvot* [commandments]". But even the members of this committee, for all their dedication to making something out of tragedy, were confused regarding the actual victims' identities. Like many others, they had simply assumed that the victims had all been Mercaz HaRav students. So when they came to Israel a few months later to set up the framework for their event, all they actually did was sign Mercaz HaRav onto their project. After their return to the U.S. they commissioned a special curriculum for the lead-in to the *yahrtzeit*, an original song dedicated to the event, and worked on the myriad technical details that needed attention. It was only sometime later that the complexity of the situation became clear to them.

After contacting Mercaz HaRav, the B'Lev Echad people understood that the yeshivah would contact the families. At various times, I heard rumors about receiving a Torah scroll from some of the Yashlatz staff, but nobody from Mercaz HaRav ever spoke to me about any plans for any event. The American organizers were frankly embarrassed when they met Rivkah Moriah for the first time in the U.S. and discovered that she had no idea about any of their plans. The first time that I talked to Rabbi Yaakov Shapiro, who had been appointed *rosh yeshivah* only a few months previous to the massacre, was the first time that I had contact with anybody from the Mercaz HaRav staff. I initiated contact with him a short time after we, the families, met to discuss the *yahrzeit* plans. We spoke briefly on the phone about the upcoming memorial and I questioned him about the upcoming event. Rabbi Shapiro told me that he had spoken with the donor and had stressed the importance of donating the scrolls to the families themselves. The yeshivah would only serve as a venue for their presentation. He thought the families had been consulted and was incredulous that no one from the yeshiva had been in touch with me since the attack. Rabbi Shapiro had also assumed that the decision to hold the event late in the afternoon of the actual anniversary (thus enabling the live feed to the U.S. to be shown midday on the same date) was made with the families in mind. On the Jewish calendar, the new day begins at sundown, not midnight, so the families would be able to use the evening before the event and most of the following day for private commemoration. By the end of our short chat, it was clear to me that Mercaz HaRav already had a firm set of plans in place for the entire event and that no one had consulted the parents in drawing them up.

My impression was that the yeshiva had assumed that the gift of a Torah scroll to each family in its son's memory was something that would be so appreciated that the details of the installation event would be of lesser importance to the families. Mercaz HaRav was acting, as they saw it, in good faith—helping each family receive a quite expensive memorial. Any public relations benefit that they might reap from the event itself did not negate the value of what they felt they were doing for us.

At the time, however, it seemed to some of the parents that Mercaz HaRav was intent on capitalizing on the donor's generosity as a means of self-promotion. Even those of us with a less adversarial view of things felt that we should have been consulted about the plans for what was shaping up to be a big tent event. This was the first anniversary of *our* children's deaths. How could anybody plan something for us on this day without first getting our input? One of the families had already been deeply hurt by a real slight to their dead son's grandfather at Mercaz HaRav and another was busy portraying them as a nefarious bunch of self-aggrandizers interested only in cashing in on our tragedy. Neither of these families wanted much to do with Mercaz HaRav —but this grand event memorializing our children was going to be held *there*. The question was, after hundreds of thousands of dollars had already been spent and more committed, what could be done?

I discussed what was going on with the shadowy anonymous donor's twenty-something representative whose number I had been given. After our phone conversation, it was clear to him that things were not going as his committee had envisioned. He decided to travel to Israel so that he could get a firsthand impression of what was happening to their well-intentioned memorial plans. Soon after, the sincere young man arrived, pencils sharpened and laptop at the ready, with a plan to meet each of the families individually and file his report back in New York. The American committee had imagined an event directed at the widest possible international English-speaking audience. Aside from wanting to gift each of the families a Torah scroll, they also wanted to highlight their carefully prepared program of Torah study. Their idea was to use the deaths of our children to focus on worldwide Jewish unity. "One people—One heart". Out of sorrow, strength. And so on. It would soon become clear to them that Mercaz HaRav did not really share their vision.

The families had set up a meeting with Rabbi Shapiro at Mercaz HaRav to discuss the *yahrzeit*. The young man from the US spent a day talking to most of the families, and came along to the meeting as well. We were all politely ushered into a rather spartan office. Rabbi Shapiro, the yeshivah's administrator, and two other senior rabbis sat down on one side of a well-worn, large formica desk and we seated ourselves on threadbare sofas and hardback chairs facing them, ready to discuss our concerns. We each, in a few sentences, took a turn expressing our thoughts. I told those assembled that the planned event was interfering with how I wanted to mourn my son on the anniversary of his murder. Others added their thoughts while Rabbi Shapiro sat in what seemed to be an almost regal silence before abruptly leaving the room.

And then the bomb went off. One of the rabbis launched into a diatribe claiming that the attack had occurred here, in his house. He told us in no uncertain terms that they were going to commemorate this tragedy, *their* tragedy, as they saw fit, in accordance with the mandate the donor had given them. Glowering at our young American friend with his laptop, the rabbi told him that the yeshivah had no need to justify itself to anyone—and certainly not to the likes of him. This yeshivah elder dismissed the months-earlier clash with his former colleague and slain student's grandfather as the doing of a few overly-emotional students and saw no need for the yeshivah to apologize for anything. Using the Hebrew second-person plural *you*, he accused the entire group of slandering the yeshivah.

Then the second rabbi asked to speak. By way of a rabbinic homily he harshly admonished us for wasting the *rosh yeshivah's* time and energy. He condescendingly likened us to bickering children and advised us that the only solution was to listen to our "father," by which he meant Rabbi Shapiro, who would make the best decision for all of us. To my ears, this was an especially surprising metaphor, since this "father," until he met me face-to-face a few minutes before the meeting, couldn't match my face to my name. Nor did he know the murdered boys.

We were all quite shocked at the tone that this meeting had taken, but in keeping with Israeli custom, individual parents returned fire, giving as good as they got. Soon the room took on an atmosphere which in another time and place would have been a prelude to a good old-fashioned brawl. I was insulted that this rabbi had thrown out a general accusation of slander, and demanded to know to whom and what he was referring. One mother asked how he dare compare the yeshivah's "tragedy" to ours. Another stormed out, declaring her disgust with their "lies."

After things had cooled down a bit, Rabbi Shapiro returned. He was troubled that things had gotten so far out of hand but also hurt by the accusations which he felt had been leveled unfairly against his school. He was conciliatory but, I think, knew that this mega-event was going to be a cornerstone for his yeshivah's much needed fundraising and couldn't afford to let it go. He also knew that with only the short amount of time remaining until the *yahrzeit*, not much could be changed anyway. Contracts had been signed, money already committed. He told us that the only concern voiced by any of the parents which he felt needed addressing was mine—that the planned event would interfere with my own mourning—but he didn't know exactly how to solve this problem.

The meeting with the yeshivah's staff ended with no real conclusion. We, the parents, sat back down together to discuss what we should do. This was the most difficult, most fraught gathering of the mourning families that there had been. On one side were those who felt estranged, for one reason or another, from Mercaz HaRav. Rivkah was adamant that she would never step foot in there. Another family felt that without acknowledgement of their previous hurt, they couldn't comfortably participate in another Mercaz HaRav event. On the other side were families who felt deeply connected to the place where their sons had studied and breathed their last. They wanted to commemorate their sons' memories on the very spot where they had lost their lives.

I felt for both sides. I had no particular ax to grind against the yeshivah in whose library my son had been killed, although I was upset by the way the evening's proceedings had gone. Receiving a gift in my son's memory worth thousands of dollars was something I didn't particularly covet—but I understood that for some of the other families having a Torah scroll dedicated to their murdered child was very important. It was traditionally the most sacred of memorials. What would happen if some of us refused to take part at all? This seemed to be a very real option—an option that would destroy the real but ethereal solidarity between us. The pain that each of us carried over his or her own loss weighed much more heavily than the mutual bonds born only out of the circumstantial tragedy which we shared.

A compromise was suggested wherein the completion of two of the scrolls, that dedicated to my son and another boy, would take place in Yashlatz and not in the Mercaz HaRav building. Thus anyone not wanting to step foot in Mercaz HaRav could at least participate in this part of the ceremony.

I felt torn, but also resentful that I was being somehow manipulated into taking part in someone else's grandiose "Worldwide Celebration of Jewish Unity." What irony. I wanted to be with close friends and family at this awful time of remembrance, not part of a crowd. If we had been consulted first, a lot of unnecessary anguish could have been avoided. I was annoyed and upset that I needed to be worrying about someone else's event, instead of concentrating on my own plans for remembering my son.

I was candid with the organizer's representative: there were only two reasons why I was going to participate. First, I knew that this event was important for some of the other families. They wanted something big. They felt it was meaningful for their sons' deaths to be publicly memorialized and broadcast to thousands. I didn't want to interfere with that. And second, painful as it was, I had to be honest with them and myself: part of me feared that if I didn't show up, my son's stepfather would be the one to carry the public mantle of memory for my son, my Avraham David. It was a thought I just couldn't stomach.

As the weeks passed and the date for the memorial grew near, I spoke several times with the young New Yorker who had visited us, as well as with another of the donor's representatives here in Israel. They were sincerely concerned about our feelings, yet sure that after so much money had been spent, the show would go on. In a sincere effort to make amends, Rav Shapiro also visited each of the families in order to smooth things over and hand-deliver the invitations to the event. I talked to Rabbi Shapiro about the importance of including my son's friends throughout the event and about other logistical concerns: where we would pray *minhah* (the afternoon service) before the event, babysitting for smaller children. He assured me that he would take care of everything. He did, and since then I've come to appreciate his humor and wisdom. I have invited him to our home and had the opportunity to enjoy his Torah discourses.

And so, after an emotionally fraught period, during a time that would already have been tension laden enough, my family and I arrived at Yeshivat Mercaz HaRav. My wife had literally shuddered at the thought of being in the library where most of the victims had been murdered. It was there that the writing of most of the scrolls was to be completed. As agreed upon, the completion of our scroll would take place at Yashlatz, in the high school's study hall. I, though, had decided that I wanted to pray in the library beforehand—as close as possible to the exact spot where my son's blood had stained the floor. After the *minhah* prayer, we gathered around a table in a corner of Yashlatz's cleared-out *beit midrash* to complete the scroll.

Once again, we found ourselves in the midst of a festive event. A group of the American organizers had flown in and hovered around wearing specially printed B'Lev Echad sweatshirts. Some had walkie-talkies. Dozens of people wandered about. Televison and film crews floated past us. Radio correspondents asked for a few words. For some reason, the scribe who wrote our scroll never arrived to complete it. Luckily, a close friend of mine who is also a scribe had come to join us. Akiva, whose Shabbat table had always had an extra space for me in my bachelor days, who had known my son since birth, who had written the parchments in the *tefillin* (phylacteries) which I purchased for his bar mitsvah, completed the scroll which was to be dedicated in Avraham David's memory. We sat together talking, as various rabbis, friends of my son, and assorted politicians and dignitaries came up to hold the quill and inscribe a letter on the smooth white parchment. My girls had left to play with other young children in an apartment across the street. Later my wife would tell me that the apartment belonged to David Shapiro, the IDF officer who had shot Abu Dheim.

After a not-unpleasant hour and a half in the Yashlatz *beit midrash*, the last lines of the Torah were completed. Before the ink had time to fully dry, an organizer from B'Lev Echad bearing a crackling walkie-talkie told us that it was time for all the fathers to gather in the Mercaz HaRav library for a group picture and then begin the procession. We blew on the ink, wrapped up the scroll, dressed it in its mantle and I carried it down a hallway that connected the high school *beit midrash* with the yeshivah library. One of the event planners, his eye on the clock, moved us quickly along for the photo-op. In the library sat the other fathers—each holding a scroll. We greeted each other as we were posed by the photographers and flashes flashed.

Then, with a sense of urgency born of international timetables and webcasts, we were told that it was time to leave the yeshivah and start the ceremonial procession outside. Carrying the scroll in my arms, my son and older daughter by my side, I exited the library—into a seething sea of humanity the likes of which I have never seen. It was like being sucked into a vortex. While we had been quietly ensconced in the *beit midrash* completing the scrolls, thousands upon thousands had gathered in the yeshivah's courtyard and on the streets below. We were instantaneously surrounded on all sides, buffeted in every direction by the throng, as we half-walked and were half-pushed down into the street to the awaiting *hupah*. Old Sephardic women, who must have been waiting for a long time to get such prime positions, pulled at the scroll's mantle, kissing it and crying out "Holy, holy, holy." They grabbed my hand as well, pulling it to their lips to kiss: I was the holy father—a relic on display. It freaked me out.

Down the steps, into the streets, pushed upon from all sides, I clung onto the scroll, scared that it would fall, while shouting at my son over the din to help his younger sister who seemed in danger of being trampled. Music blaring, yeshivah boys jostling up against us, we were moved by the unstoppable tide. My son valiantly held his sister close, trying to keep her safe as time after time we were nearly knocked over by the horde pushing in against us. It was actually frightening to think what might happen if my seven-year-old fell. At times, cradling the heavy scroll in one arm, I pushed back, hard, with the other hand—shoving people away to clear some space for my children. Holy, holy, holy?! I couldn't imagine anything further from it than this noisy, crushing parade .

At one point a friend of my dead son appeared, wearing an official event tee shirt, and he carried my terrified daughter to the relative safety of the sidelines. My son and I, wet with sweat, bruised and stepped upon, soldiered on through the streets of Kiryat Moshe wishing only to arrive at our destination already.

Finally, we made it back to the yeshivah. Inside, another mass of humanity was dancing to too-loud music and we joined them. Compared to outside, this packed crowd was a relief. I was able to lift the scroll above my head and stretch my aching arms. My son's *kippah* had long ago disappeared and someone found him a wool watch cap to stick on his head. None too soon, exhausted, we were seated alongside the other fathers on the dais as the speeches began. I begged for someone to bring us water. It took several minutes for the message to make it across the crowd, but eventually bottles were passed over the heads of the assembled crowd and we drank, thankful that the worst was over. Afterwards, the scrolls were locked up in the ark and we descended the stairs for a meal and a few more speeches. Binyamin Netanyanu, now Prime Minister-elect, again made an appearance. My son got to shake his hand. It made his evening.

For others, though, the evening went less well. It seems that the live broadcast was something of a fiasco. English speakers were missing from the program, audio feeds didn't work, screens went blank, sponsors were not acknowledged. Members of the committee were upset, some even incensed. They had worked hard at creating an event which would turn our loss into a gain for the Jewish people at large. Mercaz HaRav, though, had designed an evening which they dubbed *Zokhrim U'Mamshikhim*, We Remember and Carry On (donations gladly accepted). For the yeshivah, the event was supposed to focus on memorial, on helping the families of the victims of the massacre. And the yeshivah saw itself as one of the affected families. As the rabbi had told us, the massacre had occurred in their house. They too were mourning a loss, attempting to move on in the wake of personal tragedy. Their program featured Hebrew speakers— prominent Mercaz HaRav alumni who could offer them solace, who could remind them of better days. They were interested in the families, but also in consoling their own constituency in their own time of need. America interested them less. It was far away and the realities of American-Jewish education were foreign to them. To whom did this tragedy truly belong anyway?

Six weeks later, when my parents were visiting Israel for the Passover holiday, we installed the scroll that we had received into our synagogue in Efrat. Avraham David was a meticulous public reader of the Torah and many in the community remembered his beautiful cantillation. A Torah scroll was a beautifully fitting memorial. But…the tensions surrounding the way which we had received it still haunted me.

Perhaps those who poured so much time and money into creating this multi-media event may look at my attitude as ill-mannered ingratitude. Maybe it is. I wrote to the donor on the day following the event:

> *I know that the tragedy of the death of my son and the other seven boys hit people in such a viscerally strong way that they felt compelled to do something with their own shock and pain. I hope that the event which you sponsored helped the Jewish world deal with the loss of eight youths. I hope that it did add some light to our too dark world.*
>
> *I know that the scroll will be used weekly in my shul where my son was a frequent layner [reader] himself. All those who use it will remember something of his smile, his meticulous layning, his diligence in Torah and mitsvot. Those memories will certainly lighten their lives and ours.*

I meant it. I hope it offered some solace to the masses. I was grateful to receive a Torah scroll. Seeing people read from it every week reminds me of my son, and others in the community have expressed the same sentiment. But, if I had been asked in advance about the plans, I would have said that being part of such a grandiose undertaking would only make a difficult day even more so. I would have passed.

The way things played out was no comfort for me; it was

an ordeal. But, for the reasons I explained above, I chose to participate. What helped me through it were the efforts I had expended elsewhere to create my own way to mark a year of horrible loss.

CHAPTER SEVENTEEN:
RAIN

Only love can make it rain...

PETER TOWNSHEND, "LOVE REIGN O'ER ME"

One of my life's regrets is that despite my love of music, I have only been blessed with very rudimentary talents in that field. Notwithstanding my own failings, I have at different times played the trumpet, hosted a jazz radio program, busked on the streets playing my harmonica (together with some friends who are real musicians) and spent large amounts of time just enjoying all sorts of music. Avraham David's homeroom teacher in his last year at Yashlatz happened to be the son of a well-known klezmer clarinetist, Moshe Berlin. Moshe, in addition to paying the rent by playing weddings and the like, has been instrumental in preserving many authentic hasidic melodies and bringing them to new and wider audiences over his decades-long career. Elyashiv Berlin, his son and Avraham David's teacher, was a drummer. He often played with his father. His students would sometimes attend a wedding and discover, "Hey, that's our teacher in the band!"

A few weeks after the massacre, Elyashiv approached me with

the idea of holding a memorial concert in Gush Etzion, the region south of Jerusalem where we and the Avihayils live. This was the first memorial event suggested to me that felt worth expending energy on. I contacted several musicians I knew, rented a local hall, printed up posters, and during the week of Passover we staged a moving concert.

Over the summer, my friend and rabbi, Rav Menahem Froman, together with the Hebrew University Student Union, organized another memorial concert. This concert featured a number of prominent Israeli musicians, mainstream record-selling artists, who appeared together in the boys' memory before a full house of university students. The evening opened with a short film featuring gruesome pictures from the night of the attack. Then, as a representative of the victims' families, I addressed the crowded auditorium and tried to express to the students my thoughts about what makes song unique.

I emphasized the difference between normal speech, in which different voices compete, and song, where they can harmonize. Even in the face of tragedy, song and music can help join people together in ways that even the most carefully crafted speech cannot.

As we sat listening to the music, one musician's moving singing brought me and my wife to tears. Yonatan Razel, a classically trained pianist, composer, arranger and vocalist, played from the heart and touched us deeply. A few months later, I asked him to headline the *yahrzeit* event I was planning in my son's memory.

Even before I became embroiled in the unpleasantness surrounding the big event at Mercaz HaRav, I knew that the *yahrzeit* period would be difficult. Both the yeshivah and high school were planning memorial ceremonies to be held a few days before the actual anniversary. Protocol required putting in an appearance at too many places, listening to too many speeches. I wanted to build some type of enclosure for myself and family that would carry us through the anniversary, a life raft on which to float through the choppy waters of painful and crowded memorial services planned by others. I wanted to be able to invite people to something meaningful, something moving, something powerful that would serve both as a fitting memorial and a means of closure to an awful year. I wanted to create an event of my own. One where I could talk of my own loss, one where I wouldn't have to fight over my son's memory.

But I couldn't do this on my own. After hearing Yonatan play over the summer, I knew that one of the keys to such a memorial would be his music. I began the slow process of working my way through the layers of management that surround all modern performers in order to enlist him in my cause. Money for the hall, advertising, and countless other incidentals needed to be arranged. I spoke with different organizations, seeking sponsorship, and eventually secured funding from the Jewish Agency and some friends. I got an old acquaintance, violin virtuoso Yehoshua Rochman, to play the opening act. Moshe Berlin would follow with a short set and the main event would be Yonatan Razel. Rav Froman would also be on stage, offering his commentary to the music.

On Friday afternoon, four days before the actual anniversary, I met with the sound engineer at the hall to set up the mikes, feeds, and cables. And on Saturday night, in a torrential rain storm that came at the tail end of a winter of drought, hundreds of people began to fill the hall.

As the rain came down outside, I stepped up on the stage to, coincidentally, say something about drought and rain.

Avraham David was born in Jerusalem just after the end of the fall holidays and just a day before the blessing asking God for rain is added to our daily prayers. I remember seeing the year's first drops fall outside as his mother was in labor. The very first rains of the world are described in Genesis as awaiting both God's command and Man's need for them.

> *No plant of the field was yet upon the earth, and no grass of the fields had yet sprouted, for God the Almighty had not brought rain upon the earth and there was no Man [Adam] to work the soil (Genesis 2:5).*

The Talmud adds it own interpretation to this picture.

> *Rav Asi puzzled: It is written (Gen. 1:12), "the earth brought forth grass" on the third day; but also (Gen 2:5) "no grass of the fields had yet sprouted" on the sixth day. This teaches us that the grasses had grown and stood just below the surface [of the earth], until Adam came and requested mercy for them. Then it rained and they sprouted forth. [This is] to teach us that the Holy One desires the prayers of the righteous.*

In the Holy Land, the rains are God's precious gift. They come to us in answer to our prayers; in response to our request for God's mercy. They are the very expression of God's mercy. But we need to ask for them. We left Egypt, a land where the overflowing Nile nourishes the earth. But here in Israel our water comes "from the rains of heaven." Here, in the land that God's "eyes are upon," rain is His gift, bestowed when we love Him "with all our heart and soul" (Deut. 11). This past year we have experienced a severe drought and watched as our aquifers slowly dried up. The prayers of eight righteous young men, boys who devoted themselves to the study of God's word, were missing this year. Their voices were no longer heard among those who beseeched the Holy One to shower his blessings upon us. The ground dried up, cracks in the earth showed where once grass grew.

And I, as the Psalmist wrote, "I groaned, each night my bed swam in tears, I melted it" (Psalms 6:7). How much water rained from my red eyes, thinking about my son, feeling the terrible pain of loss. Remembering how much blood, in place of water, soaked the earth that evil night.

But this night, I want to also recall the mercy that God, and my friends and neighbors, have rained down upon us all. This is a night to reflect on loss and to ask for God's mercy, in the place of those who can no longer ask. The verse in Genesis says *"Ve'adam ayin"* -- and there was no Man, no Adam. ADaM, my precious son, *A*vraham *D*avid *M*oses, ADaM is not. He and his friends are gone and can no longer beseech God.

I need the Holy One to help heal the hole torn in my heart a year ago. Let heaven and earth once again meet; let the earth once more be kissed by God's presence. Let once more the bounty of His promise spring forth from our too-dry land. Let the cracked surface of my soul feel the warm, healing rain of God's love.

Let God's mercy rain down upon us all. *Rahamei shamayim.* Let us listen to the sounds which will envelop us this evening, and help us open our hearts to God above. And like Rav Asi taught, let us pray for what we need: *rahamei shamayim*. The mercies of heaven. *Rahamei shamayim.*

And as I wept, the music began.

I was fortunate that the concert was recorded live by Arutz Sheva, a Jewish news website aimed at a religious Zionist audience. Over the next few days, I watched and listened again and again. The music, which came from a heartfelt place, touched me deeply. It was an event which required an investment of much energy and money. But it was one of the few things that I did over the year that was actually healing. It was a salve which nurtured my broken heart with the beauty and power of sacred sounds, not the jarring noise of too-loud canned music or off-key oratory. The evening wasn't somebody else's idea of what my son was, or what I felt, or what my family and I needed in order to move on. It was *my* gift to the hundreds of people who attended and who were able to listen together with me, in memory of my son. The music washed over me and my family, over us all, and gave me strength to move through the following days that brought the year of mourning and memorial to a close.

ON MY STEPSON[*]
BY LEAH MOSES

The first Shabbat after I married Avraham David's father, I knew I was in trouble. When the time came to light Shabbat candles, I realized I had no idea where Avraham David was. I looked up and down the whole house, and he was nowhere to be found. I was frantic, trying to figure out how I would tell my new husband that I had lost his eight-year-old son.

The sun was going down, so I briefly stopped my search to make the blessing on the candles. As I finished my blessing, I heard a little voice singing out "amen." Avraham David had hidden himself in our futon couch – and had been right by my side the whole time!

The next week I started saying a special *tehinah* – prayer – for stepmothers. Divine help, I figured, was what I needed, and a prayer from our tradition was the way to ask for it. I've said this prayer every Friday night for the past eight years and given it a lot of thought.

In this *tehinah*, Rachel, our Matriarch, is referred to as the ultimate stepmother – someone all stepmothers can look to for guidance and inspiration. The idea of Rachel in this role confused me. After all, although Rachel had given her handmaid Bilhah to Jacob so that she could "also have a son," Rachel is never described as having a

---

[*] *This piece originally appeared in a memorial volume dedicated to the eight murdered boys, Princes Among Men, which was a project of Yashlatz's Class of 2008.*

relationship with the children that resulted, Dan and Naftali. When Jacob presents his family to Esau, Dan and Naftali are introduced as Bilhah's sons, not Rachel's. How could I learn from a woman who seems to have had no relationship with her stepchildren how to have a relationship with mine?

It was only through an in-depth study of our matriarch Rachel in Genesis that I came to understand her as a stepmother, and learn how I could emulate her.

When Rachel demands of Jacob, "… give me children or I will die," Jacob becomes infuriated, replying "Can I play God? It is He who is holding back children from you." Rashi, citing the Midrash, explains that Rachel was, in fact, asking Jacob to pray on her behalf that she should have children.

Jacob's anger, according to both the classic medieval commentator Rabbi Moses Nahmanides and the 19th-century hasidic work *Mei HaShiloah*, was triggered not because Rachel asked him to pray for her to have a child, but rather, by how she asked and why she wanted that child. Rachel was trying to manipulate Jacob to use his clout as a *tzaddik* to demand a child for her from God. Thus her dramatic demand, and her threat of death. And why? Not to build up the tribes of Israel, but rather, simply because Rachel "was jealous of her sister." According to the *Mei HaShiloah*, Rachel had to rectify her motivations. Children are not a means to satisfy our needs or bolster our egos. In addition, we can not allow ourselves to act badly, even if the bad behavior flows from a place of honest pain.

In giving Bilhah to Jacob, Rachel put the needs of the family before her ego.

That we see no relationship between Rachel and Bilhah's children after Rachel names them is, I think, evidence of a further clarification of motive on Rachel's part. The hardest part of being a stepmother is fully internalizing that you are not the mother. The stepchild is in your house to be with his father, and he already has a mother who loves him. A stepmother's job is to support those relationships in any way she can – any interaction that comes after that, any independent relationship that develops, is secondary. I think we see no relationship between Rachel, Dan and Naftali because Rachel realized that what the boys needed was their parents, and she backed off.

Our mother Rachel's process of detachment and clarification of motive has guided me through my step-parenting of Avraham David. On the one hand, he was always a child to be proud of. Not just smart, but clever. Pious, considerate of others, and increasingly thoughtful as he got older. I was impressed by how consciously he was choosing what kind of person he wanted to become. On the other hand, he was also very stubborn. He was endowed with a strong sense of justice, persistence, and a touch of mischievousness. These can be challenging attributes in a child in your home. A stepmother has to constantly detach, remember that it's not about ego, and watch how she behaves. (In my case, there were definitely times that I was more successful, and times that I was less so.)

My *tehinah* ends by saying that Joseph and Benjamin were Rachel's reward for having been a stepmother. It says that her children brought her "*nahat*, joy, without boundary in this world and in the world to come." Again, this is an idea I pondered for a long time. Rachel died in childbirth, when Joseph was still a young child, and she never lived to see Benjamin grow. How much joy could she have had in this world from her children?

In the months that have passed since the death of Avraham David,

I have been remembering. I remember his bright blue eyes in his shining face the first time I met him; the time he gave his little sister his ice cream cone just because she was crying that she wanted it; the time he staggered home, red-faced, carrying a case of bottled water that weighed almost as much as he did – because it was on sale, and a better bargain than just one bottle; his coming home from yeshivah and clearing the table without being asked; when he recited *mishnayot* to keep himself from hearing gossip. My memories of him are an endless source of joy -- the loss and pain, the brevity of the time he was part of my life don't matter. My stepson Avraham David Moses was a precious gift in my life, a source of joy without boundary. His tragic death in no way diminishes that.

ON MOURNING AND CONSOLATION

By **Rabbi Shimon Gershon Rosenberg** *

W hat does it mean to comfort a mourner? Can somebody actually console another for his loss? At times, the shivah comes to resemble a party—people come and go, chatting about the day's events. They do not know how to confront death. The usual questions—how did it happen, how long was he sick—these are mere subterfuges aimed at masking the fact that the one being mourned is gone. His absence is difficult to grasp. But it is also threatening, it raises feelings of guilt—why him and not me? For some, this is too much: they come to dread death like a contagious disease, a taboo never to be mentioned.

But this misses the main point. When we are confronted by

---

* *Rabbi Shimon Gershon Rosenberg, known by the acronym Rabbi ShaGaR, was an exceptional Israeli rabbi, teacher and writer. I was privileged to have been his student and English translator. He died in 2007 at the age of 57. This piece was written on the occasion of his father's death. I translated it soon after my son's death.*

another's mortality, we often react instinctively with denial. So, for example, when visiting a terminally ill patient we often avoid talk of death so as not to upset the patient. Sometimes the sick person himself is also in denial. But this is a great loss—here is the last opportunity *to* talk. After a certain point, the time comes when the most important moments of a life, ending as it must, are there for the taking. Even after death, sometimes the mourners speak only factually about the deceased, without addressing the person he or she really was.

I would like to offer some thoughts on death, thoughts that lie somewhere between the emotional and philosophical, in an attempt to go beyond the usual empty phrases bandied about in the face of loss.

Often the context of mourning offers a canvas upon which some people (especially those who see themselves as representing Judaism) paint their discussions of the soul's immortal nature. This is supposed to be comforting. But they are mistaken. They ignore the fact that death, even though first brought into the world as a curse, is an integral part of life itself—in fact, death is one of the most important parts of life. It is a mistake to imagine that the soul's continued existence can be understood in simple physical terms, in the way we might imagine the continued existence of a table.

We need to leave behind what philosophers call "metaphysical thought" because it merely confuses the matter. What do we mean by the soul's immortality? Certainly not a continued physical existence which corresponds to how the deceased was known to us before his death. We cannot make an *object* out of the deceased. Perhaps in this world, there is something of an object in each individual, but in the world-to-come this physicality, this "objectness" is stripped away—what remains is pure subject, the essence of the soul.

In life, intimacy arises only when we talk *to* someone, to his essence, and not *about* him. It is only then that the subject is created; the subject cannot come into being through indirect communication. The creation of the subject necessitates that we leave reification behind and not relate to others as objects. In death, the physical object has been removed. The deceased is no longer here. And so we need a new type of speech, one that will allow us to speak with the deceased, to remain in intimate contact with him even after his physical departure.

We are often most comfortable thinking in physical terms—the afterlife is described as an actual place, whether high in the heavens or deep below the earth. But we need to let go of such thinking. Maimonides explains that humans want immortality, but they also want flesh and blood. Unfortunately, the two are incompatible. Immortality cannot be physicality.

Medieval scholars asked why we should mourn at all if after death the soul not only lives on but even progresses to a much better place. But this question itself is evidence of the kind of confused thinking which we need to abandon. We should not think that some actual thing, some object remains after death. Death is real in this sense—it destroys that "something," the physicality of life. It is only when we confuse the soul's continued existence with something physical that we wonder why we should mourn in the face of death. Mourning lies on the physical plane—the place where death strikes.

Real discourse between people creates a relationship which is not erased even by death. We can even talk with those who have departed this world. Lubavitcher hasidism developed this into a regular practice. The last Rebbe regularly visited his father-in-law's grave and held weekly discussions with him. Somebody who was very close to you can, in fact, continue to speak through you. You can still hear him, not only with your imagination, but in a very real way. The soul's immortality needs to be understood as discourse with the subject, and not the object; with some*one*, and not some*thing*.

Each of us meets death at some point in time. The question is whether the deceased remains "someone" for us, or fades into a mere "something." The presence of the deceased is not imaginary; it can be more real than that of the living. Presence is more than mere physicality.

This brings us to consolation. Comforting mourners means giving expression to an intimacy which is not dependent upon anything—certainly not mere physical presence. When this intuition is expressed—through words, a handshake, tears—something beyond value is exchanged. This is not the place for playacting; real faith in this intuition is needed in order to give it expression. It requires no small measure of bravery to transmit.

In the case of one who has died tragically before his time, there is something beyond pain. We feel injustice. But we cannot ignore death itself. It is what provides us with the deepest intimacy, the strongest of bonds between men. Our Sages referred to caring for the dead as the only "true mercy" there is. If a man lived forever he would not be a man. The very fact that we live in the shadow of death creates our humanity. We need to confront death as something real, not an illusion; but also to realize that that which died – the ephemeral physical self – was that which in fact never existed. What is Real cannot die. By this I mean the essence of soul, that which is created through intimate interpersonal communication. If, before our deaths, we succeed in attaining this level of interconnectivity with others, that will live on. This is what can comfort us.

When one discovers that his death is imminent, he may react with denial. Many remain in this state. Others, however, move on to fear. But after fear comes acceptance. It is at this stage that the path to intimacy can be opened. It can be opened via the path of speech—the very stuff out of which the soul is made. I mean this in a very real way. The soul is created—not in a physical sense—but in a very actual sense—out of communication.

This is confusing; naturally, we confuse the Real with the physical. Of course there are tears and mourning—mourning gives expression to our humanity and it cannot be ignored; it is, in fact, a precondition for love. Only mortality gives us a sense of urgency without which we would languish, never moving forward in our daily lives with the things that really matter.

We are constantly accompanied by our thoughts about those no longer with us—even if we do not dwell upon them daily. A broken heart is a part of our lives. What comforts us is faith in something more fundamental than this. We do not need to seek a cure for our pain. When a loved one dies, our life changes forever, no matter if he is young and we are old. Our life changes, but not necessarily for the worse. The deceased is constantly with us and it is always possible to return to the relationship, to turn to him. This is what mourning is about. This is a double movement: on the one hand mourning, on the other consolation. Consolation means allowing space in our lives for our pain: not by way of anger or depression, but on the contrary, by giving our lives deeper meaning, by bringing a courageous sublimity to our interpersonal relations.

I really do not know how to deal with the death of a murdered youth. Anyone can mouth the words, but to deal with something means being able to say those words truthfully. In the face of a tragic death, it is difficult for someone from "the outside" to say anything truthful or authentic. Only one who has been there himself can speak. We should only say to another that which we can say to ourselves; otherwise our words are mere lies. We can only speak out of *existential* truth; even if what we want to say is true—first we must say it to ourselves. Only afterwards can we speak these words to another. This may still be quite difficult, nearly impossible, but when we arrive at this point —we can soften even the harshest of blows.

A youngster's death is disturbing; it shakes us out of the complacency of our daily lives. It remains as a tumor within us—but it can be changed from a malignant growth to one that can heal. I once knew a woman whose husband was killed only a few years after they married and she remained alone for the rest of her days, never remarrying. Was she truly alone all those year? Not necessarily. She remained with her late husband throughout her daily life, throughout the years of raising their children.

To speak of an actual presence may seem like apologetics, like false words of comfort. But such consolation can be real and such words can be spoken in a way that gives true comfort. This is faith at its best: Can we look at life as something positive, as something inherently good, despite the tragedy which has literally torn us apart? Will our pain continue to seethe within and destroy our lives? Or can it enrich us?

This is the most personal of choices. It cannot be made with any outside help. In moments of suffering one need ask oneself how he will mourn. The question is whether we take our tragedy back into our lives, into the rest of our relationships, and make them better. This can also be how we complete our relationship with the deceased, even if we never attained a measure of true intimacy while he lived. Our intimacy with others can be an expression of our continued connection with the deceased. Our answer is not an outright "yes" or "no." Rather, we move back and forth on a continuum – sometimes rising above the pain, and sometimes sinking into doubt. These extremes are not as important as the middle ground where we most often find ourselves. Do we have enough moments of ascendancy that they can even enlighten times of despair? There are always times of depression, of lost clarity and conviction—that is part of being human. But the greatness of our humanity lies in our ability to refuse to let these difficult moments define us, to seek instead to rise above them. This is what injects a glimmer of eternity into our midst.

10054593R0011

Made in the USA
Charleston, SC
03 November 2011